DK SMITHSONIAN HANDBOOKS

HORSES

HORSES

ELWYN HARTLEY EDWARDS

Photography by
BOB LANGRISH

A Dorling Kindersley Book

LONDON, NEW YORK, MUNICH,
MELBOURNE, and DELHI

Project Editor Jo Weeks
Project Art Editor Amanda Lunn
Designer Deborah Myatt
Editor Helen Townsend
Production Caroline Webber
U.S. Consultant Sharon Ralls Lemon
U.S. Editor Charles A. Wills

First American Edition, 1993
Reprinted with corrections, 2000
Second American Edition, 2002
6 8 10 9 7

Published in the United States
by Dorling Kindersley, Inc.
375 Hudson Street
New York, NY 10014

A Cataloging-in-Publication record
is available from the Library of Congress
ISBN 978-0-7894-8982-1

Computer page makeup by
The Cooling Brown Partnership, Great Britain
Text film output by The Right Type, Great Britain
Reproduced by Colourscan, Singapore
Printed and bound by South China Printing Company in China

see our complete product line at
www.dk.com

Contents

AUTHOR'S INTRODUCTION

To the untrained eye, breeds of horses and ponies appear to resemble one another so closely that there seem to be barely distinguishable differences between them. To the equestrian, however, the innate variations of height, conformation, and temperament between breeds are obvious. In the Eyewitness Handbook of Horses, *readers will find a comprehensive guide to identifying and appreciating all members of this fascinating kingdom.*

THE MOST APPARENT divisions among equines are between the heavier coldbloods that originated in northern Europe and the light swift hotbloods from the desert climates of North Africa and the Middle East. Because horses were for so long almost entirely the product of their environment, the influence of climate on natural selection was certainly the major factor in shaping basic types of equines. This effect is easily seen in the development of ponies; equines that were forged through a natural habitat in which a harsh climate, sparse vegetation, and rugged terrain allowed only hardy wily, sure-

MUSTANGS IN THE NEVADA DESERT
These feral mustangs are descendants of Spanish horses, which were much influenced by the "hot" Barb blood of North Africa.

footed animals to flourish. Both the differences forged through environmental factors and the types designated through domestic use are recognized in this book. Equine breeds are divided into ponies, light horses (both for riding and driving), and the draft horses, with further subdivisions by geographical origin. Finally, a section is devoted to equines in the category of types, rather than of a specific origin.

DEFINITIONS

To use this book, it is vital to understand some basic definitions, such as what is meant by a cold-, warm-, or hotblood; what constitutes a breed; and how a breed differs from a type.

CONNEMARA PONY
The surefooted, incredibly hardy Connemara derives its special qualities from the inhospitable environment of its natural habitat.

HOT, WARM, AND COLD

The Arabian – and to a lesser extent the Barb – is the fountainhead of hotblooded horses. These light-boned, quick animals evolved in desert climates and are known for volatile temperaments. Heavy draft horses such as the Clydesdale and Percheron, with large, strong bodies and calm temperaments, originated in the environment of northern Europe and are designated coldbloods. Horses in which the strain of hot- and cold-blooded ancestors are mixed, such as the American Quarter Horse and the Trakehner, are known as warmbloods. The contri-bution of the Arabian to other breeds, including the hotblooded Thoroughbred, the warmblooded Spanish Horse, and even the coldblooded Percheron, cannot be overstated.

ARABIAN

BARB

SPANISH

THOROUGHBRED

WHAT IS A BREED?

The designation of a breed relies on an organization that registers horses of a fixed type with common ancestry in the breed's studbook. In most cases, a horse must be born of parents belonging to that breed and exhibit typical breed characteristics. The breed society keeps track of horses bred selectively for consistency in respect to conformation, size, action, and, in some cases, color. Although many breeds have existed with a fixed type over a long period of time, only a few can boast organizations with records dating back more than 100 years. Prior to selective breeding, a breed constituted a band of equines inhabiting a particular area. Shaped by their environment and interbreeding, these animals naturally possessed similar characteristics. Such breeds that possessed the genetic power to pass on their characteristics (known as prepotency) have shaped the modern equine species.

WHAT IS A TYPE?

Equine types, such as hunters, hacks, cobs, and polo ponies, do not qualify as breeds because of the variation in their makeup. For example, a hunter may be any horse that is used for hunting, such as a Thoroughbred, Welsh Pony, or a crossbred. The definition does not take into account any fixed requirements of conformation, temperament, or action.

COB AND RIDING PONY
The heavy-bodied cob is built for strength; the lighter riding pony is bred for elegance.

STUDBOOKS

Two types of studbook
exist: open and closed.
In closed studbooks,
stock can be registered
only if both parents are
already registered.
Conversely, in open
studbooks stock can
be registered that is
the progeny of pedi-
greed parents of a
different breed, as
long as the animal
nominated for regis-
tration meets the breed society's
requirements. Many Warmblood
societies have open studbooks.
Although this allows breeders to tailor
their horse to meet market requirements, it can result in a loss of fixed
type. The Arabian is a prime example of
the result of a pure, closed studbook.
With an unmistakable appearance, it
transmits its inherent traits with a
consistency that would be impossible if
other strains were allowed to intermix.

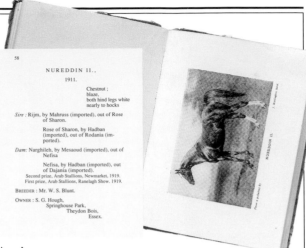

STUDBOOK
*A page from the British Arab Horse Society
Stud Book. Wilfrid Scawen Blunt, breeder of
Nureddin, was the first President of the AHS.*

THE AIM OF THE BOOK

As this book cannot guarantee readers
the ability to recognize immediately
the breed of every horse they see
(this naturally would be impossible,
because of the myriad crossbred
horses in existence), it is the purpose

EVOLUTION

This book pays attention to the world's
most influential breeds, but also delves
much further, tracing the evolution of
the equine species. From the Dawn
Horse of the Eocene period, *Eohippus*,
to such primitive horses as the Asian
Wild Horse, the Tarpan, and the heavy
Forest Horse, the book shows the
sources of all equine breeds and types.

PRZEWALSKI'S HORSE (ASIAN WILD HORSE)

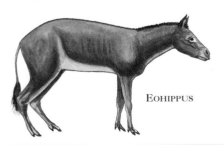

EOHIPPUS

of the book to give a broad insight
into the incredible range of horse and
pony breeds throughout the world,
while providing an unequaled
explanation into their history. While
this is a truly remarkable goal, the
Eyewitness Handbook of Horses is truly
a remarkable book.

HOW THIS BOOK WORKS

THIS BOOK is arranged according to the four major divisions of horses: ponies, light horses, heavy horses, and types. Within these four divisions, the entries are arranged by country of origin, beginning with Scandinavia, then northern and southern Europe,

northern Eurasia, Australasia, India, and, finally, the Americas. Each entry gives detailed information, in words and pictures, on the history, breeding, and characteristics of the particular equine. This annotated example shows how a typical entry is organized.

environment that has had most influence on breed •

approximate date of breed's origin •

hot-, warm- or coldblood, • depending on history of breed

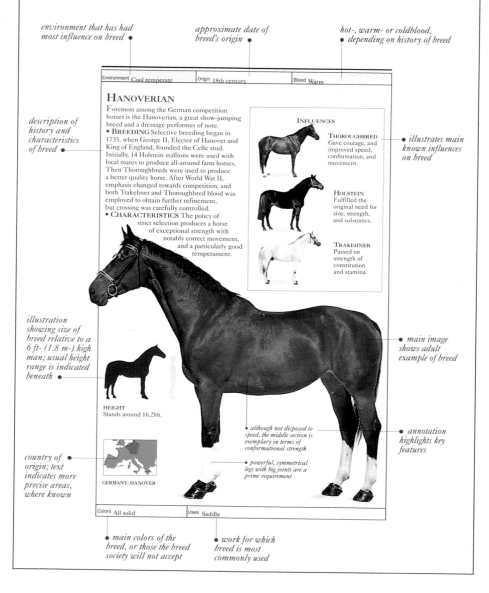

Environment Cool temperate	Origin 18th century	Blood Warm

HANOVERIAN

Foremost among the German competition horses is the Hanoverian, a great show-jumping breed and a dressage performer of note.
• **BREEDING** Selective breeding began in 1735, when George II, Elector of Hanover and King of England, founded the Celle stud. Initially, 14 Holstein stallions were used with local mares to produce all-around farm horses. Then Thoroughbreds were used to produce a better quality horse. After World War II, emphasis changed towards competition, and both Trakehner and Thoroughbred blood was employed to obtain further refinement, but crossing was carefully controlled.
• **CHARACTERISTICS** The policy of strict selection produces a horse of exceptional strength with notably correct movement, and a particularly good temperament.

description of history and characteristics of breed •

INFLUENCES

THOROUGHBRED Gave courage, and improved speed, conformation, and movement.

• *illustrates main known influences on breed*

HOLSTEIN Fulfilled the original need for size, strength, and substance.

TRAKEHNER Passed on strength of constitution and stamina.

illustration showing size of breed relative to a 6 ft- (1.8 m-) high man; usual height range is indicated beneath •

• *main image shows adult example of breed*

HEIGHT
Stands around 16.2hh.

country of • origin; text indicates more precise areas, where known

GERMANY: HANOVER

• *although not disposed to speed, the middle section is exemplary in terms of conformational strength*

• *annotation highlights key features*

• *powerful, symmetrical legs with big joints are a prime requirement*

Colors All solid	Uses Saddle

• *main colors of the breed, or those the breed society will not accept*

• *work for which breed is most commonly used*

THE HORSE FAMILY

IN 1867, A SKELETON was found in Eocene rock in the southern USA. This was *Eohippus*, and equine development can be traced from it, over a period of 60 million years, to the emergence, about one million years ago, of *Equus caballus*, the forebear of the horse. *Eohippus* was about the size of a fox, with four toes on the front feet and three toes on the back feet. Its coat was probably blotched or striped to blend in with its environment. As marshy lands gave way to treeless plains, the descendants of *Eohippus* adapted. From America, they spread across the world, via the land bridges that existed before the Ice Ages. Then, 8–10,000 years ago, the horse became extinct in America, until its reintroduction by the Spanish *conquistadores* in the 16th century.

DEVELOPMENT OF THE HOOF

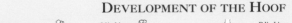

Eohippus   *Miohippus*   *Pliohippus*

Mesohippus   *Merychippus*   *Equus*

The multitoed feet of *Eohippus*, suitable for marshy ground, adapted as conditions changed. *Mesohippus* had three toes while *Merychippus*, which had longer legs, made use of only the central toe. *Pliohippus*, emerging some six million years ago, was the first single-hoof equine, and was equipped for survival in the savanna-type conditions of the Miocene period.

EPIHIPPUS

EOHIPPUS   MESOHIPPUS   MIOHIPPUS   MERYCHIPPUS   PLIOHIPPUS

OROHIPPUS

ASINUS

EQUUS

SKULLS

Early horses had short-crowned teeth, suitable for browsing. As their food changed, their teeth adapted to enable grazing on abrasive grasses. The neck lengthened so that the head could be raised higher and the animal could graze at ground level. In addition, the position of the eyes altered, allowing all-around vision.

Eohippus

Mesohippus

Miohippus

Merychippus

Pliohippus

Asinus

Equus

ZEBRA

After the land bridges disappeared, the striped species of *Equus (Equus zebra)*, were distributed throughout southern Africa. Three subgeneric forms remain: Grevy's, Mountain, and Burchell's Zebras.

ZEBRA

ASS

Equus hemionus hemionus, the wild ass, and the related subspecies, are found in western Asia and the Middle East, the swift Onager occurring particularly in Iran.

ASS

DONKEY

The domestic ass, the donkey *Equus asinus*, was originally distributed throughout North Africa. From there it has spread to many countries and is common throughout Europe.

DONKEY

MULE

The mule is a hybrid, a cross between a jackass (male donkey) and a horse mare. The less usual cross between a horse and a female donkey (jenny) is a hinny, regarded as inferior in strength to the mule.

MULE

PRZEWALSKI'S HORSE		
TARPAN	PONY TYPE 1 PONY TYPE 2 HORSE TYPE 3 HORSE TYPE 4 (SEE P.14)	MODERN
TUNDRA		
FOREST HORSE		

MODERN BREEDS

Man has developed the modern horse, by means of selective breeding, to produce stock that will be well-equipped to meet the purposes for which it is required.

PRIMITIVE HORSES

FOR MOST of the Ice Ages, *Equus* moved into Europe and Asia from the Americas. The process stopped about 10,000 years ago when the horse became extinct in the Americas. Four primitive horses evolved in Europe and Asia, according to their environment. In Asia, there was the steppe horse, *Equus przewalski przewalski poliakov*, now known as the Asian Wild Horse or Przewalski's Horse; farther west the light-limbed plateau horse, *Equus przewalski gmelini antonius*,

the Tarpan, developed; and in northern Europe, the heavy, slow horse, *Equus przewalski silvaticus*, the Forest or Diluvial Horse, evolved. In northeast Siberia there is evidence of another primitive horse, the Tundra Horse.

PRZEWALSKI'S HORSE

The Asian Wild Horse is found in zoos, but there are moves to reintroduce it to its wild Mongolian habitat. Its heavy, convex-profiled head and upright mane are distinctive. Its chromosome count is different to the domestic horse – 66 as opposed to 64.

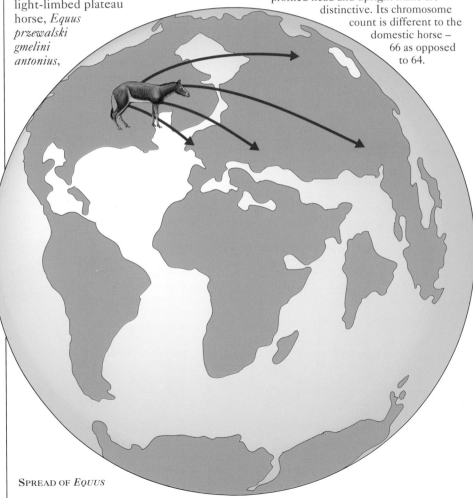

SPREAD OF *EQUUS*

TARPAN
The swift-moving Tarpan is slim and lightly built. Its dun coat resembles that of a deer, and turns white in winter. There may be a connection between Tarpan and Arabian root stock. Technically extinct, the Tarpan survives in a herd maintained at Popielno, Poland.

FOREST HORSE
The extinct Forest Horse appears to have been a massive, thick-legged, browsing animal. It was large-hoofed, enabling it to live in the swamps, and had thick, coarse hair, which was probably dappled for camouflage. It is thought to be the ancestor of the European heavy horse breeds.

TUNDRA HORSE
The remains of what may have been the Tundra Horse, along with those of mammoths, have been found in the Yana valley in northeast Siberia. The local Yakut ponies, with their thick, white coats, are held to be its descendants. Otherwise, this fourth primitive does not seem to have had any direct influence on equine development.

KEY

TUNDRA

FOREST

TARPAN

PRZEWALSKI

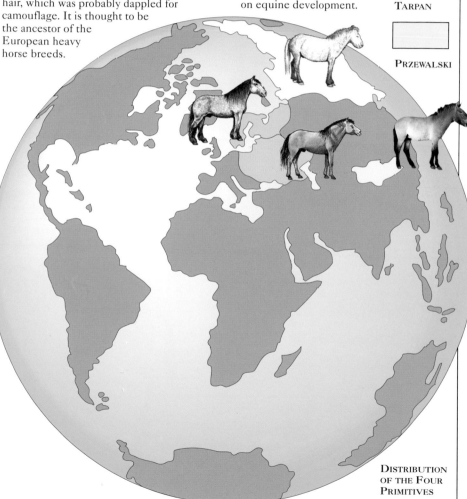

DISTRIBUTION OF THE FOUR PRIMITIVES

POSTULATED HORSE TYPES

DURING THIS CENTURY, Professors J.G. Speed of Edinburgh, Edward Skorkowski of Cracow, and Hermann Ebhardt of Stuttgart made detailed analyses of early equine bone structure, dentition, and other evidence. They concluded that a further four sub-species of *Equus* existed prior to the domestication of horses in Eurasia some 5–6,000 years ago. These were called Pony Type 1, Pony Type 2, Horse Type 3, and Horse Type 4. The nearest modern equivalents of each are: Pony Type 1 – the Exmoor; Pony Type 2 – the Highland; Horse Type 3 – the Akhal-Teke; and Horse Type 4 – the Caspian.

PONY TYPE 1
From northwest Europe, this pony stood between 12 and 12.2hh and had a straight profile, broad forehead, and small ears. It was highly resistant to wet and able to thrive in harsh conditions. Remains in Alaska show a jaw formation similar to the Exmoor's.

PONY TYPE 2
From northern Eurasia, this type was between 14 and 14.2hh. Heavily built and coarse in appearance, this animal had a heavy head and convex profile, and resembled Przewalski's Horse most closely. It was resistant to cold and vigorously prepotent.

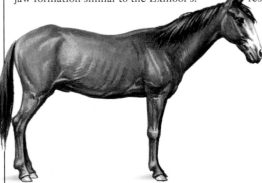

HORSE TYPE 3
From central Asia, this animal was about 14.3hh, was lean and thin-skinned, with a thin neck and fine ears, a long and narrow body, and a goose-rump. It was resistant to extremes of heat and was capable of surviving in desert conditions.

HORSE TYPE 4
From western Asia and thought to be as a prototype Arabian, this horse stood between 10 and 11hh, and was very refined and slimly built, with a small head and concave profile. The tail was noticeably high-set. A desert or steppe horse, it was resistant to heat.

MODERN EQUIVALENTS

The four postulated types are obvious derivatives of the early primitive horses (see pp.12–13), bringing us a step closer to the modern breeds. Pony Type 1, for example, has its present-day equivalent in the Exmoor (p.72), which still retains the peculiar jaw formation. The Highland (pp.66–67) clearly owes something to Pony Type 2, although it is the Asiatic Wild Horse that is most similar. The Akhal-Teke (pp.176–77) has all the characteristics of Horse Type 3, while the Caspian (pp.88–89) is closest to Horse Type 4.

KEY TO MAP

The four horse and pony types occurred principally in those areas (shaded on the map) in which the early horse-cultures evolved, particularly the Middle East and Asia, spreading outward from those regions.

PONY TYPE 1

HORSE TYPE 4

PONY TYPE 2

HORSE TYPE 3

PONY TYPE 2 & HORSE TYPE 4

PONY TYPE 2 & HORSE TYPE 3

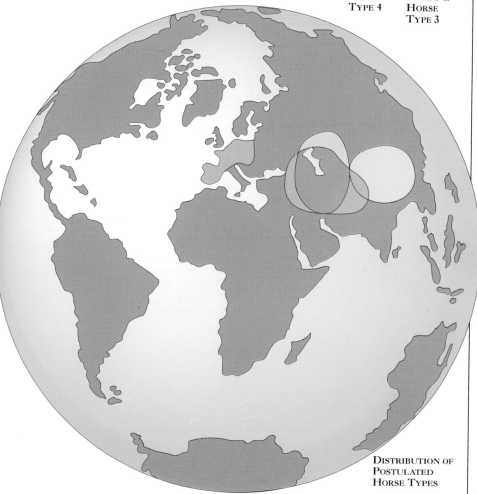

DISTRIBUTION OF POSTULATED HORSE TYPES

ARABIAN, BARB, AND SPANISH INFLUENCE

THE GREATEST IMPACT on the development of the world's breeds was made by the hugely prepotent Arabian horse. It was supported by the genetically powerful Barb of North Africa, which in turn was responsible for the equine race's "third man," the Spanish Horse. This latter breed dominated Europe between the 16th and 18th centuries, and laid the foundations for the American breeds. The evolution of the Thoroughbred in England in the 17th and 18th centuries is credited to the import of "eastern" or "Arabian" sires. However, Barbs, Spanish Horses, and swift native stock provided the basis for the English "running horses," which made possible the development of the Thoroughbred.

ARABIAN

The Islamic *Jihad* of the 7th century was as much a watershed in equine as in human history, as it ensured the spread of the Arabian horse into the Iberian Peninsula and eventually Europe. Within 120 years of the death of the Prophet Mohammed, the Muslim empire extended from China to Europe. The steppe horses, spreading

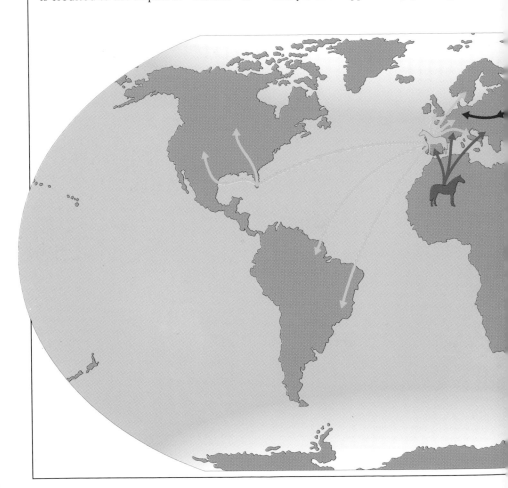

outward from Asia Minor, were all influenced by Arabian blood, and by that of other "oriental"-type hotbloods, such as the Akhal-Teke and Turkmene. These horses are closely linked with those of the Arabian Peninsula.

BARB

In the 7th century, the Berber horsemen pushed into Spain from North Africa, there-after thrusting upward to Gaul. The Moorish invasion of Europe was halted by Charles Martel and his Frankish knights at Tours in AD 732, but by then the presence of eastern blood was sufficiently well-established to become a principal influence in Europe and the foundation for many of the present-day breeds.

SPANISH

The Spanish Horse was the premier horse of Europe for over two centuries, and the favored mount of kings and captains. Its influence was pervasive and remarkable. In the early 16th century, Spanish Horses were taken to the Americas by the *conquistadores*. There they founded breeds that remain with us, the indelible imprint of Spanish blood still apparent. Few of the European breeds are without the Spanish influence, which extends into the Lipizzaners of the Spanish School and underpins breeds such as the Friesian and Welsh Cob. Although the Spanish Horse was not noted for its speed, it combined great strength with exceptional courage and fire.

KEY TO MAP

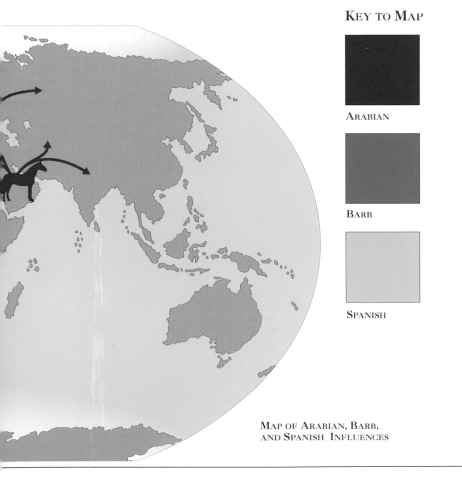

ARABIAN

BARB

SPANISH

MAP OF ARABIAN, BARB, AND SPANISH INFLUENCES

CONFORMATION

GENERALLY, "CONFORMATION" is used to describe the shape or form of a horse. More specifically, conformation is concerned with the structure of the skeletal frame. Conformation is the sum of component parts and their relationship, which contributes to the overall perfection of an animal.

In well-made horses, no single feature is exaggerated or so deficient as to disturb the general symmetry. What constitutes "correct" conformation is governed by the work the horse is bred to do. Well-made, proportionate horses, of whatever type, are able to perform work more efficiently and over a greater period of time. There is less risk of strain because no single part of the structure receives excessive or disabling wear as a result of being overused. The balance and athletic qualities are greater, and potential performance is higher, because the limbs function to their full capacity.

HORSE SKELETON

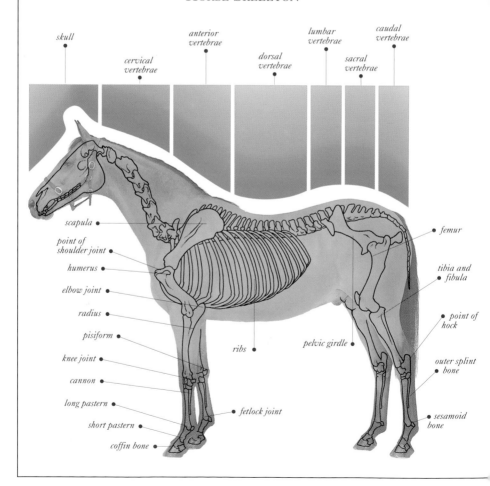

skull

cervical vertebrae

anterior vertebrae

dorsal vertebrae

lumbar vertebrae

sacral vertebrae

caudal vertebrae

scapula

point of shoulder joint

humerus

elbow joint

radius

pisiform

knee joint

cannon

long pastern

short pastern

coffin bone

ribs

fetlock joint

pelvic girdle

femur

tibia and fibula

point of hock

outer splint bone

sesamoid bone

POOR CONFORMATION

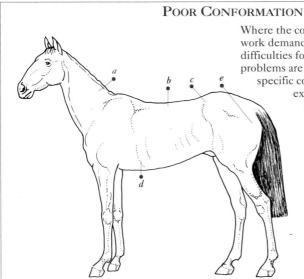

Where the conformation is unsuited to the work demanded, and thus creates physical difficulties for the animal, temperamental problems are also likely to occur. The specific conformational failings exhibited in this example are: the inclination to a "ewe neck," causing bitting and carriage difficulties (a); a long, weak back structure (b); slackness through the loin (c); insufficient depth of girth (d); and weak quarters (e). All these deficiencies contribute to an inefficient mechanical structure and increase the likelihood of strain and disease in the component parts.

POINTS OF THE HORSE

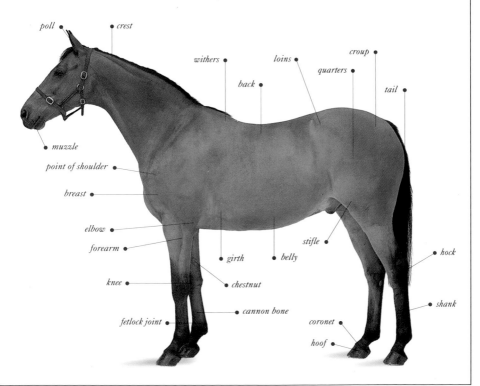

poll • crest • withers • loins • crop • quarters • back • tail • muzzle • point of shoulder • breast • elbow • forearm • stifle • hock • girth • belly • knee • chestnut • shank • cannon bone • fetlock joint • coronet • hoof •

LIFE CYCLE OF THE HORSE

THE AVERAGE equine gestation period is 11 months and a few days. Within half an hour of being born, the foal will be on its feet and nuzzling the mare for its first feed. Once on its feet, the foal, although unsteady, is able to follow its dam (mother). Mares reach puberty at between 15 and 24 months. They can breed from two to three years old, although four is more acceptable. Males are often sexually capable as yearlings, but in domestic conditions they are not used as stallions before three to four years. Mature at five to six years, the horse can live for 20 to 30 years or more.

FIRST 12 MONTHS

The young foal has long legs in proportion to the body, a natural defense against predators in the feral state. Foals are able to eat solid food at six weeks. At two months, the foal loses the furry milk hairs and, in domestic conditions, will be weaned from its dam when between four-and-a-half and six months old.

1 YEAR OLD

FOAL

AGEING BY TEETH

At birth a foal has no teeth; the central two incisors cut through the gums at ten days old. By the time it is six to nine months, the foal has a full set of milk teeth. A full set of permanent teeth are in place by five to six years. A horse's age can be judged accurately by its teeth up to the age of ten, but after this it becomes more difficult.

ADULT JAW
Each jaw has 12 molars and six incisors. Males have additional "tushes" between the molar, and incisor teeth on each jaw.

LATE YEARS

The joints may become puffy as the circulation becomes less effective, and the effects of work become evident in the legs. Old horses often stand "over at the knee." Hollows sometimes develop over the eyes, and the back may dip more than usual (a "sway" back). The teeth become worn with age and chewing becomes difficult. The digestive process is also less effective and it may become difficult to keep the horse in a good and healthy condition.

OVER 20 YEARS OLD

YEARLING

A Thoroughbred horse, bred to mature quickly, becomes a yearling on the first day of the January following its birth. The age of non-Thoroughbred horses is usually accepted as being taken from May 1. At 12 months, the young horse is still leggy and somewhat uncoordinated in its movements, but the frame is beginning to fill out, a process that continues up to maturity, when the highest point of the croup will be in line with the withers. Up to that time, the croup is noticeably higher, the horse "coming up in front" by gradual stages as it gets older. The last points of growth in the horse are the epiphyses, the "growth plates" on the long bones of the legs. Until these are closed, the leg is not capable of sustaining the effects of hardwork, particularly under weight, without the risk of the leg being damaged or becoming mis-shapen. The epiphysis at the end of the cannon bone, above the fetlock joint, is usually closed at between 9 and 12 months. However, that at the end of the radius, immediately above the knee, does not close until the horse is between two and two-and-a-half years old.

2 YEARS OLD

3 YEARS OLD

flat, oval tables; long, small cups

JAW AT 5 YEARS
Central, lateral, and corner incisors are permanent. "Cup" marks appear.

round tables; oval cups

JAW AT 12 YEARS
Teeth slope more; the groove is about halfway down upper corner incisors.

triangular tables; rounded cups

JAW IN OLD AGE
Teeth are long and the groove on the corner teeth is hardly apparent.

MIDDLE YEARS

In the middle years (from 5 to 10 years of age), the body is fully formed, and the distance between wither and elbow is close to that of the elbow to the ground. All the internal organs are, of course, fully developed and the physical proportions are established. In a well-made horse the length of neck will be about one-and-a-half times the measurement from poll to lower lip, taken down the front of the face. At this stage in its development, the horse should be at the peak of its powers, provided the early training has been directed at the formation of the correct musculature.

10 YEARS OLD

COAT COLORS

THE ORIGINS of the varied equine coat colors lie in the individual genes, of which there are 39. They result in thousands of possible combinations of color. For some breeds, color is a prime consideration, although all breed societies insist on points such as correct conformation and movement taking precedence. Palominos, Appaloosas, and other spotted breeds, like the Knabstruper, as well as the American Pintos, Paints, and Albinos, are often considered "color breeds," despite the fact that they are essentially practical, working horses. It is interesting to note that the spectacular colorings of these breeds all derive from strains that were once relatively common in the Spanish Horse, but which no longer exist in the modern Spanish horses. Thoroughbred, Arabian, and Barb horses do not have part-colored, spotted, or palomino coats.

GRAY
Black skin with white and black hairs. Coat lightens with age.

FLEA-BITTEN
Gray coat, developing small dark specks with age.

PALOMINO
Gold coat, the color of a new penny; white mane and tail.

CHESTNUT
Reddish gold shades. "True" has lighter or darker mane and tail.

RED CHESTNUT
A variation of chestnut. Sometimes includes black hairs.

LIVER/DARK CHESTNUT
Dark, liver-colored hairs, almost the color of a bloodstone.

BLUE ROAN
Black or black-brown body, with white hairs giving a bluish tinge.

RED ROAN
Bay or bay-brown body, with white hairs giving a red tinge.

BLACK
Black pigment throughout the coat, legs, mane, and tail.

APPALOOSA

Appaloosa coloring (not all spotted horses are of the Appaloosa breed) is varied. The five principal patterns are: blanket – white over hips, with or without dark spots; marble – red or blue roan, with dark coloring on the edges of the body and a frost pattern in the middle; leopard – white with dark spots; snowflake – dominant spotting over the hips; frost – white speckling on a dark ground. Skin on the nose and genitalia is mottled with black and white spots, a white sclera encircles the eye, and the hooves are distinguished by vertical stripes.

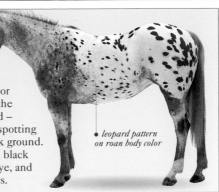

• *leopard pattern on roan body color*

BAY
Red-brown to dark brown-gold, with black mane, tail, and legs.

LIGHT BAY
A variation on bay caused by yellow or chestnut hairs.

BRIGHT BAY
Predominating red hairs give the bright bay coloring.

YELLOW-DUN
Yellow hair on black skin. Blue dun has greyish or black hair.

BAY BROWN
Mainly brown, with black muzzle, legs, mane, and tail.

BROWN
Mixture of black and brown, with black legs, mane, and tail.

DAPPLE GRAY
Rings of dark hair on a gray coat. These disappear with age.

SKEWBALD
Large irregular patches of white and any other color but black.

PART-COLORED
Skewbald refers to a coat having patches of white and any other defined color except black (see left). A black-and-white coat is called piebald. The part-colored coat of the American Pinto is described as either ovaro or tobiano (see pp.204–205).

MARKINGS

THE WHITE MARKINGS that occur on the face, muzzle, and legs are a means of positive identification and are carefully recorded in the documentation required by breed societies. In addition to the common markings, flesh marks or patches of white occur on the underside of the belly and the flank area. Flesh marks occur more frequently on the Clydesdale than on other breeds.

IDENTIFICATION MARKS

White hairs caused by saddle or girth galls are "acquired markings," as are brands and freeze marks, both of which are a means of identification – a precaution against theft. Freeze marking results in a set of identifying letters and figures made up of white hairs (or, in gray horses, black hairs). Identification marks can also be im-printed on the hoof with a heated iron. Whorls, or "cowlicks," are an irregular setting of coat hairs, also used for identification. They are permanent. Chestnuts, the horny prominences on the inside of all four legs, are like an equine fingerprint. They are individual and permanent, but are not used in identification.

STAR

STRIPE

SNIP

WHITE MUZZLE

BLAZE

WHITE FACE

LIP MARKS

BRAND MARKINGS

On horses, a brand can be used to denote ownership or identify a specific breed. The mark is made with a hot iron on the actual hide, and is perma-nent. Brand marks are made in prominent positions, like the thigh or shoulder. Normally, only one mark is made, but occasionally several brands are used, each having a different meaning. Lipizzaners, for example, have four: the stud brand, the ancestral brand, the foal brand, and the traditional brand, a simple L.

• the elk horn brand, mark of the ancient Trakehner breed

the Edelweiss • flower, with a letter "H" at its center, is the Haflinger brand

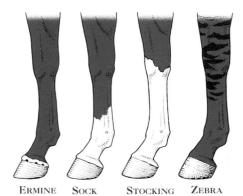

ERMINE SOCK STOCKING ZEBRA

LEG MARKINGS

Leg markings are usually white. They are: ermine marks, when the marks are around the coronet; socks, when the white extends from the hoof to the knee but does not encompass that joint; and stockings, when it extends over the knee. Zebra markings, rings of dark hair on the lower legs, are of primitive origin and were for camouflage. They are seen on breeds of great antiquity, like the Highland and the Fjord. The horses depicted on the cave walls at Lascaux, France, have these markings, and are extraordinarily similar to the Highland.

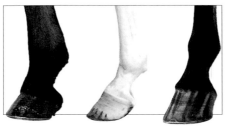

BLUE HOOF WHITE HOOF STRIPED HOOF

HOOF MARKINGS

Hooves of slate-blue horn (blue hoof) are preferred. Blue horn is considered dense in texture and very hard-wearing. Conversely, a hoof of white horn (white hoof) is thought to be soft and not able to stand up to wear well. There is no proof to support these contentions. White hooves accompany legs with white socks or stockings. The Appaloosa and other spotted horses have hooves with black and white in vertical stripes (striped hoof).

DORSAL OR EEL STRIPE

The dorsal or eel stripe extends from the tail, and is often accompanied by a band across the withers. It is almost always found with a dun coat, either yellow, blue, or mouse-dun, and there will sometimes be zebra markings on the legs.

The dorsal stripe and dun coloring are characteristic of primitive stock existing before and after the Ice Ages. The Tarpan and Przewalski's Horse have these colorings, which are also reproduced in stock having strong connections with them. The Spanish Horse included a spectacular yellow-dun strain, with black mane and a prominent dorsal stripe.

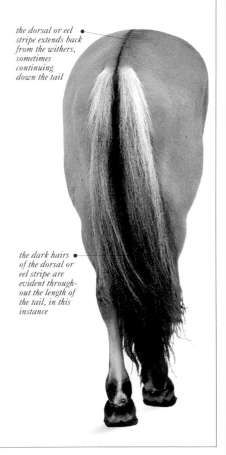

the dorsal or eel stripe extends back from the withers, sometimes continuing down the tail

the dark hairs of the dorsal or eel stripe are evident throughout the length of the tail, in this instance

PACES

THE FOUR PACES that are natural to the horse are the walk, the trot, the canter, and the gallop. The first three of these may be subdivided in accordance with modern dressage requirements. The walk, for instance, is divided into medium, collected, extended, and free. The subdivisions for trot and canter are medium, working, collected, and extended. In addition to the four natural paces, there are the specialized gaits based loosely on the amble and the pace, in which the legs move in lateral pairs. The pace, employed by modern harness-racing horses, is a faster version of the amble.

THE WALK

The walk is a pace of four beats marked by the placing of each lateral pair of hooves. When the walk begins with the left hind leg, the sequence of hoof falls is: left hind; left fore; right hind; right fore. Medium walk is the hind hooves touching the ground in front of the prints made by the front hooves. In collected walk, steps are shorter and more elevated, with the hind hooves touching the ground behind the front hooves' prints. In extended walk, the hind hooves touch down in advance of the front hooves' prints. In free walk, the whole outline is extended.

THE TROT

The trot is a two-beat pace in which one diagonal pair of legs is placed down simultaneously and then, following a moment of suspension, the horse springs onto the other diagonal pair. For instance, the first beat is as the left fore and right hind touch the ground (the left diagonal). The second is made on the touch down of the right fore and left hind (the right diagonal). At the trot, the knee is never advanced beyond a line drawn from the poll to the ground. The extremes of collection in the trot pace are the movements of *piaffe* and *passage*.

THE CANTER

The canter is a three-beat pace, the horse leading with the right foreleg when circling to the right and vice-versa. When the horse attempts to lead with the outside foreleg, i.e. right foreleg on a circle to the left, it is a "false" lead, termed cantering on the "wrong leg." The sequence of hoof falls that give the three rhythmic beats are, on the right lead: left hind, left diagonal, in which the left foreleg and right hindleg touch the ground simultaneously, and then the right foreleg – called the leading leg.

THE GALLOP

The gallop is the fastest of the four natural paces. It is usually understood to be a four-beat pace, but there are variations in the sequence according to the speed. With right fore leading, the sequence of hoof falls is: left hind, right hind, left fore, right fore, followed by a period of full suspension with all feet off the ground. A Thoroughbred gallops at 30 mph (48 km/h) or more. The leading foot touches the ground in line with the nose, even though at full stretch the hoof will be in the air in advance of that line.

SPECIALIZED GAITS

The pacing gait has two beats, which are made by the legs moving in lateral pairs (left fore and left hind, followed by right fore and right hind). The fastest exponents of the pacing gait are the American Standardbred harness racers. With the exception of the Icelandic Horse, which employs the specialized and very fast *tölt*, a four-beat running walk, other breed-specific gaits are confined to the Americas, although there are some Asian breeds that pace naturally.

A UNIQUE GAIT
The gait of the Peruvian Paso evolved over 400 years.

SPORTS AND LEISURE

SINCE PEOPLE have always enjoyed competition, horses were probably raced against each other very early in the history of equine domestication. The first recorded races, however, are those between chariots, and they preceded ridden races by many centuries.

DRIVING

Chariot racing was popular in Ancient Greece and was part of the Roman circus. The modern equivalent is harness racing. Pleasure driving, often involving the use of elegant vehicles, is more leisurely. Competitive driving trials also require a degree of elegance; they include a "Presentation" phase and a dressage test, but this is then followed by a tough and demanding cross-country marathon over 17 miles (27 km).

RACING

Racing, the "Sport of Kings," has been part of the sporting scene for centuries, but owes its modern form to the evolution of the

FLATRACING
Flatracing takes place in almost every country in the world. Newmarket is the center of British racing and Kentucky is America's "horse state."

Thoroughbred horse in 17th- and 18th-century England. Many of the famous British courses were laid out in the 18th century and the British pattern of Classic Races, such as the Derby and the Oaks, are followed in most of the countries that have a racing industry (for example, the Kentucky Derby in the USA and the New Zealand Classic Races). In Britain and Ireland, particularly, racing

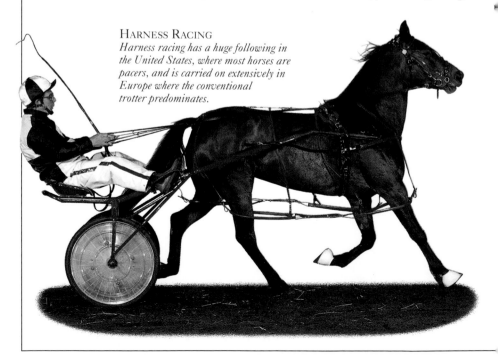

HARNESS RACING
Harness racing has a huge following in the United States, where most horses are pacers, and is carried on extensively in Europe where the conventional trotter predominates.

continues during the winter in the form of
steeplechasing over fences, the most famous
British races are the Grand National at Aintree
and the Cheltenham Gold Cup.
Point-to-point events for amateurs are held
in both countries.

DRESSAGE, JUMPING, AND EVENTING

Most modern horse sports
originated in the practices of war.
Even the formal and highly
skilful dressage test, the 20th-
century version of one of the
classical arts of the Renaissance,
derives from cavalry horse tests
carried out by the armies of
Europe in the 19th century.
But it was the Greek general,
Xenophon (c. 430–355 BC), who
first described a progression of training
and defined specific movements.

SHOW JUMPING
*Show jumping competitions were first included as
part of the Olympic Games in Paris in 1900.*

Show jumping, an enormously popular
sport, also has its military connections, the
system of "forward riding" over obstacles
being introduced into cavalry training by the
Italian Captain Federico Caprilli (1868–1907).

Eventing derives from the old "Military,"
a complete test for officers and their horses.
It involves three phases: a dressage phase, a
steeplechase and cross-country course, and
a final show jumping phase.

ENDURANCE AND PLEASURE

Endurance riding over long distances also has
a military precedent in cavalry practice, and in
its modern form is a highly sophisticated, specialized sport. Usually, the best long-distance

horses are Arabians or Arabian part-breds.
Otherwise, horses are used for the sheer
pleasure of riding in the country, whether
riding "Western" or "English" seat, while
enthusiasts in England and Ireland devote
the winter to the chase, following a pack of
hounds across country, taking their fences as
they come. Hunting also occurs elsewhere,
particularly in France and North America.

SIDESADDLE
Up to the 1920s, the majority of women
rode sidesaddle. Today, there is a
revival of this graceful art, particularly
in Britain, where there is a flourishing
Ladies' Side-saddle Association, which
organizes an annual show and holds
numerous clinics.

DRESSAGE
*Dressage is a major
discipline in Europe
and America.*

WORKING HORSES

FOR 4,000 YEARS, the horse was primarily used for the purposes of war, but there were also many peaceful uses to which it was put. Horses were used to draw loads in harness and to pull traveling chariots. Later, in the 18th and 19th centuries, horses were also used to pull light coaches and elegant vehicles, the development of which was encouraged in Europe by increasingly sophisticated road systems.

MILL HORSE
A horse-operated grist mill, commonplace up to the beginning of the 20th century.

INDUSTRY

The coming of the railroads in the first half of the 19th century may have sounded the death knell for the magnificent era of the road and mail coach but, in fact, it created greater employment for horsepower. Thousands of light horses were used for delivery work of all kinds, and drew buses and cabs in the heavily populated towns and cities. Heavy horses moved materials to and from the railheads. They were used in freight yards and for moving rolling stock, so that for

over a century the railroad companies were the biggest owners and employers of horses. The huge network of canals in Britain and the USA were serviced by barge horses, the "boaters" who drew loads of 60 to 70 tons. Mining companies used great numbers of ponies underground, and horses were needed at the pitheads to turn the windlass of the hoist, as well as to draw coal wagons. (The steam engine's power, developed by James Watt in 1769, was measured in horsepower.)

In England, well into the 19th century, Dales and Fell ponies and Cleveland Bays were still used in the British pack trains that carted lead ore from the hill mines to the Tyneside docks, while pack ponies were also commonplace all over Europe.

AGRICULTURE

Horses were also essential to agriculture through both the 18th and 19th centuries, taking the place of the slower oxen teams that had worked the land from medieval times. The agricultural cycle, from the preparation of the land, through sowing and cultivating, to the harvesting of the crop and its subsequent delivery to the consumer, was dependent upon horsepower. In the United States, the huge combine harvesters were drawn by 40-horse teams. Between 1900 and 1910, there were over 5,000 breeders of Percheron horses alone in the United States, and the number of registrations had reached a massive 31,900.

PLOWING
Up to World War II, horses played a large part in the rural economy.

MILITARY AND POLICE

Up to World War I, millions of horses were employed in the armies of the world; even in World War II large numbers were still in use. The German Army had thousands of horses on the Eastern Front, the Poles in 1939 had 86,000 horses, and the Russians a staggering 1.2 million.

Today, many nations still employ cavalry for ceremonial purposes, and no state occasion is thought to be complete without the pageantry of mounted horsemen. Police forces, too, appreciate the psychological power of the horse, and make use of

DRUM HORSE
*The Drum horse
of the British
Household Cavalry,
Blues and Royals.*

MOUNTED POLICE IN NEW YORK CITY
*New York, as well as other American cities, employs
a mounted police branch to carry out regular patrol
duties in the city.*

mounted branches for controlling crowds, and for patrolling the busy city streets, as well as park areas.

TRAVEL AND RECREATION

A worldwide industry has been built on trekking, trail riding, and other vacations involving horses. Riding schools form a significant part of the leisure industry and there is a constant demand for qualified instructors. All in all, there is still a place in society for the working horse.

DRIVING WAGON
*The gypsy wagon is almost
as old as the history of
wheeled vehicles.*

SADDLES

THE FIRST SADDLES built on a wooden frame were developed in the early Christian era by the Sarmatians, a tribe of nomads from the steppes bordering the Black Sea. They formed the basis for saddle construction up to modern times. Many saddles still use a wooden tree, now usually made from strips of laminated wood reinforced with metal plates through the frame. Some trees are molded from plastic.

KING'S
SADDLE
*The saddle
of Henry V of
England is similar to
that of the Sarmatians.*

the rear of the saddle is called the cantle, and is reinforced with light metal

stirrup leathers are made from oxhide, buffalohide, or tough rawhide, and are often reinforced with nylon

the front arch of the saddle, called the pommel or head, is reinforced with a metal head and gullet plates

saddle pads of sheepskin or cloth-covered foam give additional protection to the horse's back

the flaps of the saddle are made from strong oxhide, which is also soft and supple

GENERAL-PURPOSE SADDLE

For many riders, the general-purpose saddle is the most practical choice. The majority are made with spring trees – metal strips laid lengthways on the tree to give increased resilience. They can be used for jumping, cross-country riding, and schooling work.

SPECIAL SADDLES

Different types of saddle are designed specifically for particular pursuits. There are dressage saddles, which are cut straight in the flap to allow the rider to sit with a long stirrup leather. The forward-cut, lightweight saddle is used for show jumping. There are also saddles for show-ring classes, and long-distance riding, and very light race saddles, weighing 1 lb (450 g) or less.

RACING SADDLE
*Flat-race saddles
can weigh as little
as 8 oz (220 g).*

JUMPING SADDLE
*This is cut so that the
rider is positioned well
forward in the saddle.*

WESTERN SADDLE

The Western saddle was derived from saddles brought to America by Spanish settlers, which were adapted to the requirements of the cowboy. They are comfortable for long journeys, they can be fitted to almost any horse without risk of damaging the back, and all of the cowboy's gear can be fastened to them.

the saddle is essentially a work platform and the seat is broad and comfortable

the characteristic horn on the Western saddle acts as a post to which the lariat can be tied

the back jockey is, in effect, the panel of the saddle, the latter being put on over a heavy blanket

fenders, the equivalent of the European stirrup leather, protect the rider's clothes from being soaked in sweat

Western stirrups are often made of wood covered with rawhide, which insulates the rider's feet against cold

DRESSAGE
Fitted with long girth straps.

LANE FOX
Favored in the American gaited show classes.

POLO SADDLE
Built on an extra strong tree to allow for heavy use.

SIDE SADDLE
Originated in Europe in the 14th century.

BRIDLES AND BITS

A BRIDLE CONSISTS OF a head piece and reins attached to a bit, and provides a means of control. In general terms, bridles fall into one of five categories: the snaffle, the simplest control; the double bridle, the most sophisticated; the pelham, a compromise between snaffle and double; the gag, with an upward sliding motion; and the bitless bridle, also known as the hackamore.

SNAFFLE BRIDLE

This bridle applies pressure upward against the mouth's corners and also across the jaw, when the head is a little in advance of the vertical. The bit lies on the gum, the "bars" of the mouth, between the molar and incisor teeth. The construction of the mouthpiece can be varied to produce specific actions.

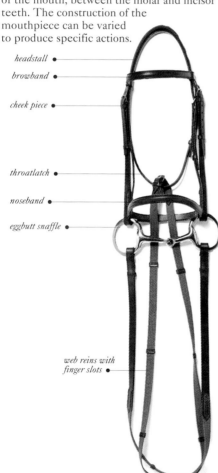

headstall •

browband •

cheek piece •

throatlatch •

noseband •

eggbutt snaffle •

web reins with
finger slots •

DOUBLE BRIDLE

This bridle applies complex pressures, allowing the rider to enforce a balanced head carriage. It is suitable for the schooled horse and rider, allowing a degree of finesse not found in other bridles. The bridoon acts to raise the head, whereas the curb lowers it causing the nose to draw back.

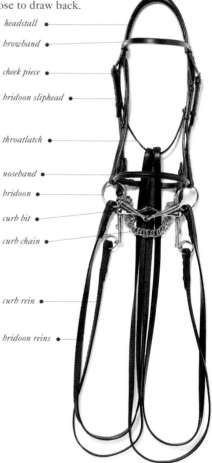

headstall •

browband •

cheek piece •

bridoon sliphead •

throatlatch •

noseband •

bridoon •

curb bit •

curb chain •

curb rein •

bridoon reins •

WESTERN BRIDLE

This bridle is dependent solely on curb action. The differences in construction (the open-end reins, for instance) are just variations in detail. The Western bridle is the culmination of a system of training involving the progressive use of carefully balanced nosebands *(bosal)*, prior to control being transferred to the bit. The method derived from the horsemanship of the Iberian Peninsula, and was brought to America by the *conquistadores*. Although the bit is potentially severe, control over a well-trained horse is exercised by minimal indications made by the expert rider's hand.

BITS

The majority of bits are made from metal – stainless steel being the preferred material. Otherwise, mouthpieces may be of vulcanite, nylon, flexible plastics, or india-rubber, all of which are softer in their effect. The mildest form of snaffle, for instance, has a rubber mullen, or half-moon mouthpiece. A joint in the mouthpiece produces a "nutcracker" action, which is more severe.

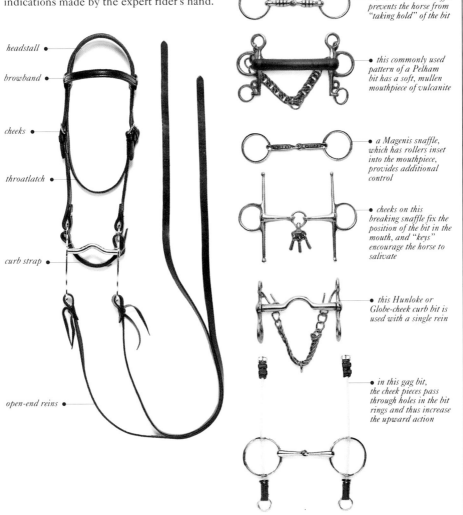

headstall

browband

cheeks

throatlatch

curb strap

open-end reins

- a roller-mouth snaffle prevents the horse from "taking hold" of the bit

- this commonly used pattern of a Pelham bit has a soft, mullen mouthpiece of vulcanite

- a Magenis snaffle, which has rollers inset into the mouthpiece, provides additional control

- cheeks on this breaking snaffle fix the position of the bit in the mouth, and "keys" encourage the horse to salivate

- this Hunloke or Globe-cheek curb bit is used with a single rein

- in this gag bit, the cheek pieces pass through holes in the bit rings and thus increase the upward action

CARRIAGES

THE FIRST CARRIAGES were chariots. These were light vehicles drawn by a pair of horses or a team of four horses abreast. The small size of the horses made riding impractical, hence the use of swift-moving, spoke-wheeled chariot formations on flat and open terrain.

The sophisticated Egyptian war chariot was established by 1600 BC and the Chinese developed a similar vehicle 300 years later. The Chinese contributed some of the most important advances in horse driving, inventing the breast harness, the horse collar, the breeching strap, and lateral shafts for single-horse vehicles.

HUNGARY

In the Middle Ages the Hungarians pioneered carriage and coach design, their forebears having swept into Europe with Attila and his armies, all supported by a sophisticated wagontrain. Hungarian craftsmen, of the Komorne area, made the first road coaches in the late 15th century. The trade was centered on the village of Kocs in the Kormone, and the coach *(koksi)* takes its name from there.

The most important feature of the Hungarian coach was that, for almost the first time in the history of vehicle

GOVERNESS CART
A member of the gig group, entrance was by the rear door.

the collar is essential for efficient traction •

the traces attach the horse to the load •

the pole, on either side of which are hitched the • *"wheel horses"*

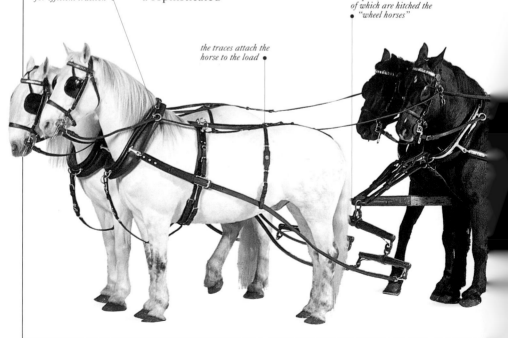

building, the front wheels were smaller than the rear ones, allowing the fore-carriage to turn on a very tight lock. Hungarian vehicles also had a lower center of gravity than their predecessors, and so could be driven very much faster. The light body, supported in leather slings like a hammock, proved to be far more comfortable for the passengers. The multi-leaved elliptical spring, another Hungarian invention, led to the coach's improved performance, increased comfort for passengers, and allowed the vehicle to be drawn safely at higher speeds.

FRENCH DEMI-MAIL PHAETON
The largest and heaviest of the phaeton family.

WESTERN COACH
The rounded body was suspended on leather "thorough-braces" to counteract the effects of rough ground.

BRITAIN AND EUROPE

The final improvements to coach design were made in Britain, largely as a result of the hard roadways established in the early 19th century, and because of the availability of Thoroughbred horses developed in the previous century. Although it lasted only until the mid-19th century, the English "coaching era" marked the culmination of a great driving tradition, and inspired "private driving," which resulted in the establishment of the huge carriage-building industry. In other parts of Europe, where roads were less advanced, the breeding of heavy, coach-type horses, deriving from the draft breeds, was encouraged.

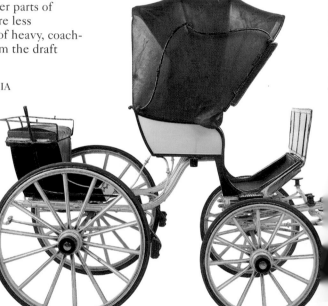

IRISH JAUNTING CAR
The passengers sat facing outwards on seats set each side of the body.

AMERICA AND AUSTRALIA

The American equivalent of the British mail coach was produced in 1825. The best models were made by Abbot-Downing Co. in Concord, New Hampshire – and were known as "Concords." In 1853 they were introduced to Australia and were successfully adapted to the local conditions.

COCKING CART
Used to carry fighting birds, it was usually drawn by two horses harnessed in tandem.

SPIDER PHAETON
The vehicle originated in America. Drawn by a pair, it was the fashionable turnout for park or town driving in the 19th century.

CARRIAGE GROUPS

There were four groups of carriages and carts: phaetons, gigs, sporting dogcarts, and breaks. The phaetons were a large family, of which the "spider" was the

FOUR WHEEL RALLI CAR
An offshoot of the dogcart, it seated four people with room under the seat for luggage.

most elegant. Gigs were vehicles that were drawn by a single horse. They were the equivalent of family cars and were much used by doctors, businessmen, and traveling salesmen. From the sporting dogcarts emerged Ralli cars, market and country carts, the traditional Irish Jaunting Car, the Governess Cart, and the Cocking Cart, so called because of its association with cockfighting. The Governess Cart, entered by a rear door, enabled governesses to take

children for drives without fear of them falling out. The fourth group, the breaks, were four-wheeled sporting vehicles which carried up to six passengers, as well as the dogs and game. A Skeleton Break was used for breaking young horses to harness, and there were other variations, such as Wagonettes used for passengers and luggage. These could be drawn by a single horse, a pair, "unicorn" (a pair hitched behind a leader), or a team. Finally, there were the char-a-bancs (cars with benches) and omnibuses.

HOODED WELL GIG
A most practical vehicle for doctors, businessmen, etc., it also provided protection against the weather.

BAROUCHE
This was the most fashionable of the larger carriages and was drawn by a pair of quality horses.

IDENTIFICATION KEY

THE BREED SECTION of this book has been divided into three main parts: ponies, light horses, and heavy horses, with a final section on types (horses and ponies that do not qualify for breed

status). This identification key follows the same structure, the main groups being described in Stage 1 (below), with the breeds then grouped by geographical location in Stage 2 (pp.44–47).

STAGE 1

THE THREE GROUPS

The main differences between ponies, light horses, and heavy horses are in weight, body build (which extends to differences in proportion), surface area, gaits (arising as a result of the conformational proportions), and, to a lesser degree, height.

Weight varies considerably between groups and also within a group: an Arabian, for instance, may weigh on average 920 lb (418 kg) and a Thoroughbred 1,066 lb (484 kg). A riding or carriage horse can be as tall as a draft breed. Ponies are

held, perhaps too arbitrarily, to be those breeds and types below 15hh.

But the real difference between the pony and the horse is one of proportion. In Thoroughbreds, the distance from wither to ground exceeds the length of the body, the legs being longer than the girth measurement. The opposite is true of the pony.

HEAVY HORSE

LIGHT HORSE

PONY

Horses and ponies are measured from the highest point of the withers to the ground. The hand measurement (hh) is medieval in origin and a hand is accepted as being 4 inches (10 cm), the approximate breadth of a man's hand. Measuring in hands is largely a British and American convention, but is the traditional form. In Europe and indeed elsewhere, however, measurement is more commonly made in centimeters – a practice likely to become universally acknowledged.

WHAT IS A PONY?

Ponies differ from horses by virtue of their unique character and size. They are deeper through the body in relation to their height, while the length of the head is usually equal to the wither-to-point-of-shoulder measurement, and that of the back from wither to croup. There is also a difference in the action, stemming from the early environment. Horses are rarely as surefooted, and they do not have such a developed sense of self-preservation, as ponies.

HEIGHT
Ponies stand between 10 and 15hh.

withers are inclined to roundness

short, strong back

thick tails and manes provide protection against cold and wet

neat head, broad between eyes, with tapered muzzle

depth through girth is characteristic

cannons are short, with more than adequate bone for the body build

hooves are hard, small, and often of blue horn

ACTION
There is noticeable knee action with strong flexion of the hocks. The foreleg then extends before the hoof touches down to give length to the stride.

head is short with very mobile, sharp, and small, pointed ears

WHAT IS A LIGHT HORSE?

The light horse exhibits conformational features that make it suitable to be ridden. The form of the back allows for a saddle to be fitted easily. The "true" ribs, the first eight, are flat, so that the saddle lies behind the trapezius muscle. The ten "false" ribs are rounded and "well-sprung." The withers are clearly defined, and the slope of the shoulders, from their junction with neck and withers to their point, is about 60°.

HEIGHT
Horses usually stand between 15 and 17.2hh.

length in the proportions of the hindquarters contributes to speed

back is not too broad, with well-defined withers

hocks are clean, large, and set low to the ground

hooves are well-formed, proportionate to the size and build

ARABIAN
Marked by a concave profile, tapering to a small muzzle.

BARB
Less quality than the Arabian, with thickness through the jowl.

ACTION
The long, low, economical action, with little bend or lift in the knee, covers a lot of ground. The slope of the shoulders is critical for producing a smooth, effective riding movement.

THOROUGHBRED
Long, lean head with a straight profile.

WHAT IS A HEAVY HORSE?

The heavy draft horse gives an impression of weight combined with strength. The body is wide and the back is broad, often accompanied by rounded withers, which in some breeds, in the interest of increased pulling power, may be higher than the croup. The body is heavily muscled, particularly over the loin and quarters. The shoulders are relatively upright to accommodate the collar, and the legs are thick and short.

HEIGHT
Heavy horses usually stand between 16 and 18hh.

back is broad and fairly short; withers are round and inclined to be flat

hindquarters are short, very wide, and heavily muscled

chest is very broad, with forelegs set well apart

FEATHER
Pronounced feathering, typical of the heavy breeds, can cause an irritative skin condition, by retaining wet soil. Clean-legged breeds are better equipped to work in deep, heavy ground.

ACTION
A short action gives maximum traction. The straight angle of the shoulders causes the forelegs to be bent at the knees, which are lifted high before the hooves are brought down.

FEATHERED   CLEAN LEGGED

STAGE 2

The following pages show all the breeds featured in this book grouped by their geographical origin, with the page reference given directly beside the breed name. Colored tint bands indicate which of the three main groups (ponies, light horses, or heavy horses) the breed belongs to. Many of the more popular breeds are to be found distributed throughout the world and, therefore, cannot be identified purely by geographical location. However, a pony at a riding stable in Iceland will most certainly be of the Icelandic Horse breed and,

ICELAND

Icelandic Horse 48

FINLAND

Finnish Horse 106

DENMARK

Danish Warmblood 114
OTHERS
Frederiksborg 110,
Knabstruper 112

Jutland 216

BELGIUM

Belgian Warmblood 124

Brabant 218

GERMANY

Oldenburg 134

Holsteiner 132

AUSTRIA

Haflinger 58

Noriker 220

FRANCE

Ariègeois 60
OTHERS
Landais 62,
Pottock 63

Selle Français 146
OTHERS
French Trotter 147,
Camargue 148,
Anglo-Arab 150

at a similar establishment in Scotland, it will probably be a Highland pony. Similarly, a heavy horse in Italy is more likely to be an Italian Heavy Draft than a Clydesdale. Of course, many horses are crossbreds, but in western countries, and others where breeding is practiced selectively, the stallions used are registered in a studbook and stamp their progeny with their own dominant characteristics. This is particularly true of Arabians, Thoroughbreds, Cleveland Bays, and many of the native ponies registered in closed studbooks.

NORWAY

Fjord **50**

Døle Gudbrandsdal **104**

SWEDEN

Swedish Warmblood **108**

OTHER
Gotland **52**

North Swedish Horse **214**

NETHERLANDS

Friesian **116**

OTHERS
Gelderlander **118**,
Groningen **120**,
Dutch Warmblood **122**

POLAND

Huçul **54**

Konik **56**

Wielkopolski **128**

OTHER
Trakehner **126**

Württemburg **136**

OTHERS
Bavarian Warmblood **130**,
Hanoverian **131**,
Rhinelander **138**

HUNGARY

Nonius **140**

Furioso **141**

OTHERS
Shagya Arab **142**,
Lipizzaner **144**

Boulonnais **223**

OTHERS
Ardennais **222**,
Breton **224**,
Percheron **226**,
Norman Cob **228**

UK & IRELAND

Shetland 64

OTHERS
Highland 66,
Dales 68, *Fell*
69, *Hackney
Pony* 70

Connemara 76

OTHERS
Exmoor 72, *Dartmoor* 73, *New Forest Pony*
74, *Welsh Mountain Pony* 78, *Welsh Pony* 79,
Welsh Pony of Cob Type 80, *Riding Pony* 241

ITALY

Maremmana 164

OTHERS
Bardigiano 82, *Salerno*
160, *Sardinian* 162,
Murgese 165

Italian Heavy Draft 236

PORTUGAL

Sorraia 84

Lusitano 168

OTHER
Alter-Real 170

GREECE

Skyrian Horse 86

Pindos Pony 87

N. EURASIA

Bashkir 90

Akhal-Teke 176

OTHERS
Budenny 178, *Kabardin*
180, *Karabakh* 181,
Orlov Trotter 182,
Don 184

INDIA

Indianbred 190

Kathiawari 188

NORTH AMERICA

Rocky Mountain Pony 96

OTHERS
American Shetland 94,
Chincoteague/Assateague 98,
Sable Island 99

Pinto 204

OTHERS
Saddlebred 194,
*Missouri Fox
Trotter* 198

MEXICO

Galiceno 100

Thoroughbred 152

OTHERS
Hackney Horse 154, *Cleveland Bay* 156,
Irish Draft 157, *Welsh Cob* 158,
Hunter 238, *Hack* 240, *Cob* 242

Clydesdale 230

OTHERS
Suffolk Punch 232,
Shire 234

SPAIN

Andalusian 166

MOROCCO

Barb 172

MIDDLE EAST

Caspian 88

Arabian 174

MONGOLIA

Przewalski's Horse 186

AUSTRALIA

Australian Pony 92

*Australian Stock
Horse* 192

Mustang 202

OTHERS
Morgan 200,
Standardbred 209

Palomino 203

OTHERS
Quarter Horse 206,
*Tennessee Walking
Horse* 208

Appaloosa 196

OTHERS
Colorado Ranger
210

SOUTH AMERICA

Falabella 102

Criollo 212

OTHERS
Paso 213,
Polo Pony 244

PONIES

Environment Tundra	Origin Pre-Ice Age	Blood Warm

ICELANDIC HORSE

Despite its small stature, the Icelandic Horse is referred to as a horse rather than a pony, and it occupies a special place in the lives of the Icelanders. Horses were brought to Iceland in the longboats of the Norsemen between AD 860 and AD 935.

• **BREEDING** Few breeds can boast such purity of blood as the Icelandic Horse. There has been no crossing with other breeds for almost 1,000 years. Selective breeding has been practiced from the earliest times, but practical breeding programs were first introduced in the principal breeding area of Skagafjördur in 1879. The quality of the breed's five natural gaits is given particular attention by breeders, as are the 15 accepted color types.

• **CHARACTERISTICS** The horses are often kept in a semiferal state and can live outdoors all year round in severe conditions. They are used for all types of work, they provide meat, and they are integral to the traditional sporting activities of the island. As well as the basic gaits, Icelandic Horses also pace (*skeid*) and move at the famous *tölt*, a fast running walk.

ICELAND

HEIGHT
Stands between 12.3 and 13.2hh.

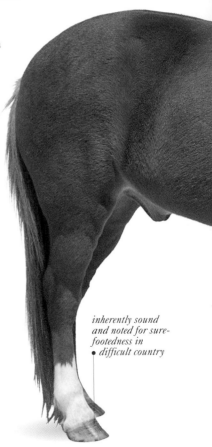

inherently sound and noted for sure-footedness in
• *difficult country*

INFLUENCES

TARPAN
Gave the breed constitutional hardiness and increased speed.

FJORD
Combined primitive qualities with some added refinement.

Colors All	Uses Saddle, Harness

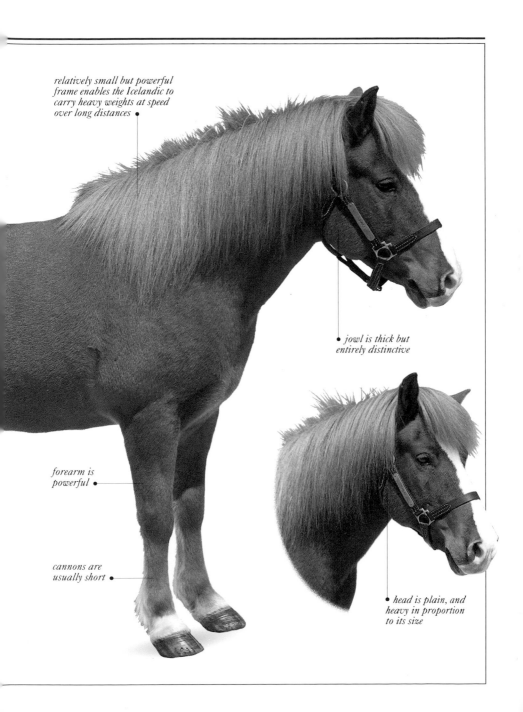

relatively small but powerful frame enables the Icelandic to carry heavy weights at speed over long distances •

• jowl is thick but entirely distinctive

forearm is powerful •

cannons are usually short •

• head is plain, and heavy in proportion to its size

Environment Taiga	Origin Pre-Ice Age	Blood Warm

NORWEGIAN FJORD

The attractive Norwegian Fjord, with its pronounced dorsal stripe and zebra-barred legs, is closest in appearance to the primitive Mongolian or Asian Wild Horse (Przewalski's Horse, see pp.186–187) from which it descends. Since Viking times, it has been traditional to cut the coarse mane so that it is erect, the central black hair standing above the rest.

• **BREEDING** Descended from Przewalski's Horse, the Fjord also has more than a suggestion of Tarpan influence. This horse of the Vikings was taken in longboats to Scotland's Western Isles and to Iceland. Bred throughout Scandinavia, but principally in Norway, the Fjord is exported to Germany, Denmark, and central European countries where its qualities of endurance and hardiness are highly valued.

• **CHARACTERISTICS** The powerful, compact Norwegian Fjord is a versatile animal. It takes the place of the tractor on mountain farms, it will plow and carry pack loads over steep tracks, and it is as good under saddle as in harness. It is economical to keep and courageous, but has a will of its own.

NORWAY

dun coloring is accompanied by dorsal stripe running from forelock to tail tip •

• *hock joints are particularly strong*

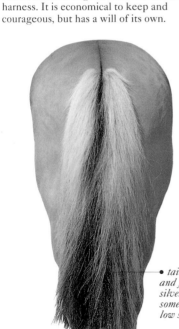

• *tail is thick and full, often silver, and sometimes low set*

Colors Dun	Uses Pack, Harness, Saddle

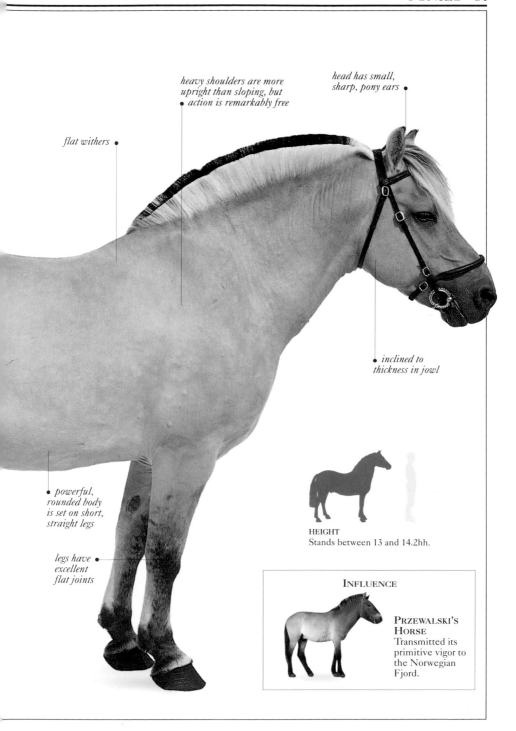

heavy shoulders are more upright than sloping, but action is remarkably free

head has small, sharp, pony ears

flat withers

inclined to thickness in jowl

powerful, rounded body is set on short, straight legs

legs have excellent flat joints

HEIGHT
Stands between 13 and 14.2hh.

INFLUENCE

PRZEWALSKI'S HORSE
Transmitted its primitive vigor to the Norwegian Fjord.

Environment Temperate, Controlled	Origin Pre-Ice Age	Blood Warm

GOTLAND

The Swedish Gotland or Skogruss Pony is probably the oldest
of the Scandinavian breeds and it retains much of its primitive
character. It once lived in a semiwild state on the island of
Gotland in the Baltic Sea and in the Löjsta forest in Sweden.

SWEDEN: GOTLAND

• **BREEDING** The ponies originated on Gotland, where they
have probably lived since the Stone Age. They are considered
descendants of the Tarpan, but Arabian blood seems
to have been introduced in the last century and selective
breeding is now practiced. Today, Gotland ponies are also
bred on the Swedish mainland.
• **CHARACTERISTICS** The Gotland was once employed
as a general-purpose farm pony, but the modern ponies are
now used for riding and are said to excel at jumping and
in trotting races. Their action at the walk and trot is quick
and active, but their movement at a gallop is not impressive.

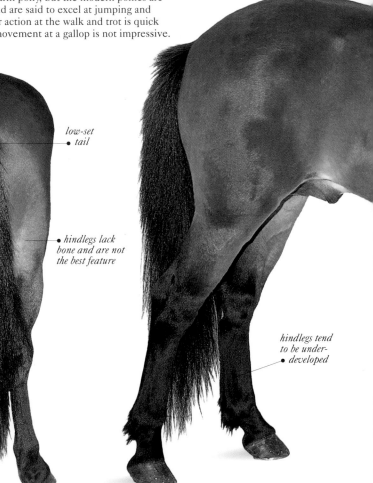

*low-set
tail*

*hindlegs lack
bone and are not
the best feature*

*hindlegs tend
to be under-
developed*

Colors Brown to Palomino	Uses Saddle, Harness

shoulders, though strong, are relatively upright

short neck

HEIGHT
Stands between 12 and 12.2hh.

frame is narrow and lightly built, but the Gotland has great endurance

INFLUENCES

TARPAN
Transmitted a primitive vigor, great hardiness, and endurance.

ARABIAN
The refining, upgrading influence improved action.

hard hooves

Environment Cool temperate	Origin Pre-Ice Age	Blood Warm

HUÇUL

The Polish Huçul is a prime example of a working horse. It is the standard workhorse in the farming communities of southern Poland and the Carpathian Mountains. Principally a harness animal used for light agricultural work, the Huçul is also used as a pack pony to transport loads over difficult mountain tracks.

• **BREEDING** The breed can be regarded as a descendant of the Tarpan, the "primitive" horse which survived in Poland until relatively recently. The Huçul originated in the Carpathian Mountains where similar ponies have existed for many thousands of years. At some stage, there was possibly an oriental influence, and the modern pony, which is bred selectively, is more refined than previously.

• **CHARACTERISTICS** The Huçul is strong, hardy, sensible, and docile.

POLAND: CARPATHIAN MOUNTAINS

quarters
slope down

selective breeding
has improved the
hindleg structure

strong, hard-
wearing legs and
hooves

Colors Dun, Bay, Piebald	Uses Harness, Pack

shoulders are
inclined to
be upright

round, flat withers

head is medium-sized,
"primitive" in most
respects, but not
without some quality

short, compact
body

HEIGHT
Stands between 12.1
and 13.1hh.

hooves are
uniformly sound
and the pony is
surefooted

INFLUENCE

TARPAN
Provided the
essential base
stock for the
modern Huçul.

Environment Cool temperate	Origin Pre-Ice Age	Blood Warm

KONIK

The Konik can be described as one of Poland's base breeds. The word means "little horse" and the Konik is, indeed, more horse than pony, even though it rarely exceeds 13hh.

• **BREEDING** The Konik is one of the few direct derivatives of the vigorous, primitive Tarpan and, as such, is of particular interest. The breed, which has inhabited Poland from ancient times, has been "improved" by infusions of oriental blood. It is officially recognized and is bred at some of the Polish state studs, as well as by numerous farmers. A uniform type has existed for many years.

• **CHARACTERISTICS** The Konik retains all the hardiness and robust constitution of its ancestor, the Tarpan, but is very quiet in temperament, easily managed, and capable of working hard on minimum rations. It is used in all forms of light agriculture, for haulage, and in harness.

POLAND: SOUTH AND EAST

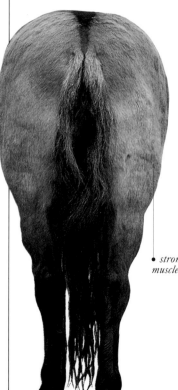

• *strong, well-muscled quarters*

strong, well-made • *hindlegs*

some feathering occurs at • *the heels*

Colors Dun	Uses Harness, Light Draft

back is compact and fairly wide

strong, short neck

forehand, with relatively upright shoulders, is well-suited to harness

HEIGHT
Stands around 13hh.

body is notably strong and there is depth through the girth

INFLUENCES

TARPAN
Passed its constitutional strength to base stock.

ARABIAN
Provided the refining and upgrading influence.

Environment Mountain	Origin 18th–19th century	Blood Cold

HAFLINGER

The Haflinger of the Austrian Tyrol is distinguished by its striking chestnut or palomino coloring, accompanied by a flaxen mane or tail. All Austrian Haflingers bear the Edelweiss brand mark with the letter "H" at its center, and they are sometimes referred to as the Edelweiss Ponies.

• **BREEDING** The center of Haflinger breeding is the village of Hafling in the Etschlander Mountains in Austria; the principal stud is at Jenesien. The pony is technically a coldblood but has an Arabian foundation sire, El Bedavi XXII. The base stock was the now extinct Alpine Heavy Horse. Huçul, Konik, and related Bosnian ponies are all genetically related to the Haflinger.

• **CHARACTERISTICS** A mountain pony, reared on the high alpine pastures, the Haflinger works easily on the steep slopes. It is ridden, used in forestry work, and will draw a sleigh or wheeled vehicle. The breed is strong and hardy and is very long-lived. Haflingers are not worked until they are four years old, but may continue to be active and healthy at 40 years of age.

AUSTRIA: TYROL

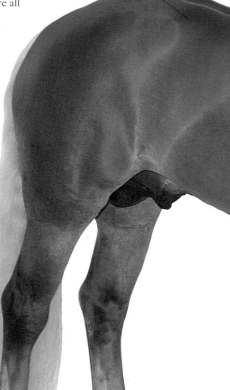

strong loins

head has lively and kindly expression, with large eyes, wide nostrils, and small, mobile ears

Colors Chestnut, Palomino	Uses Pack, Saddle, Light Draft

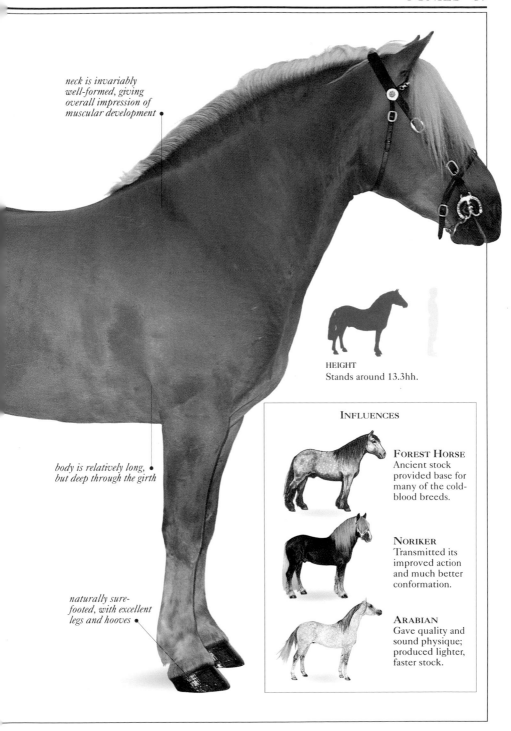

neck is invariably
well-formed, giving
overall impression of
muscular development

body is relatively long,
but deep through the girth

naturally sure-
footed, with excellent
legs and hooves

HEIGHT
Stands around 13.3hh.

INFLUENCES

FOREST HORSE
Ancient stock
provided base for
many of the cold-
blood breeds.

NORIKER
Transmitted its
improved action
and much better
conformation.

ARABIAN
Gave quality and
sound physique;
produced lighter,
faster stock.

Environment Mountain	Origin Prehistoric	Blood Cold

ARIEGEOIS

The black Ariègeois, sometimes called *cheval de Mérens*, is a true mountain pony, at home in conditions of snow and ice and impervious to the coldest weather. It is not, however, resistant to heat. In appearance, it resembles the British Fell, and is an almost exact replica of the Dales pony.

• **BREEDING** It takes its name from the Ariège river and its home is the eastern Pyrenees, which divide France from Spain, particularly in the high valleys toward Andorra. It may be the descendant of the horses depicted in the wall pictures of Ariège about 30,000 years ago. It was subsequently influenced by Roman mares and then by oriental blood.

• **CHARACTERISTICS** Primarily a pack pony, the breed can work unshod on the steep and icy mountain paths. For this reason, it was much in demand by smugglers operating along the Spanish border. It also works on the steep slopes of the upland farms where tractors are impractical. The breed is versatile, hardy, and able to work hard on minimal rations. White markings on the solid black coat are unusual.

FRANCE: EASTERN PYRENEES

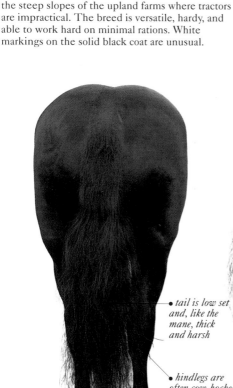

• *tail is low set and, like the mane, thick and harsh*

• *hindlegs are often cow-hocked*

Colors Black	Uses Pack, Light Draft

upright shoulders

flat withers

facial hair is thick and coarse as protection against cold

body has depth but quarters often slope from croup

hooves are so hard that they rarely require shoes, the density of the horn being exceptional

HEIGHT
Stands between 13.1 and 14.3hh.

INFLUENCES

ROMAN PACK HORSE
Base stock, added size and substance.

BARB
Gave spirit, constitution, stamina, and endurance.

Environment Cool temperate	Origin Pre-Ice Age	Blood Warm

LANDAIS

The Landais, originally semiwild, is now bred selectively to fulfill the demand for children's ponies generated by the formation of pony clubs in France. It also provides the base stock for the French Riding Pony *(Poney Français de Selle)*, a pony of greater quality following the pattern set by the British Riding Pony.

• **BREEDING** The original habitat of the Landais was the heavily wooded Landes region, south of Bordeaux. There was also a bigger strain, often termed Barthais, which inhabited the Chalosse plain where the grazing was better. Both are probable descendants of the Tarpan. After World War II, Welsh Section B stallions and Arabians were introduced.

• **CHARACTERISTICS** The modern Landais is lightly built, but hardy and easy to keep. It is said to be docile and intelligent.

INFLUENCES

ARABIAN
Gave physique along with quality and temperament.

WELSH B
Added its substance and action, to Arabian qualities.

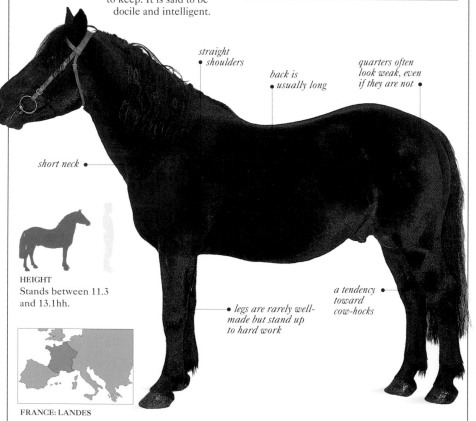

straight
• shoulders

back is
• usually long

quarters often
look weak, even
if they are not •

• short neck

HEIGHT
Stands between 11.3
and 13.1hh.

a tendency •
toward
cow-hocks

• legs are rarely well-
made but stand up
to hard work

FRANCE: LANDES

Colors Bay, Brown, Chestnut	Uses Saddle

Environment Mountain	Origin Post-Ice Age	Blood Warm

POTTOCK

The Pottock is one of the few indigenous
ponies remaining in France and is still semiwild. On the whole, it is unprepossessing in
appearance, but it is tough and very hardy.
There are three recognized types: the Standard
and the Pinto (between 11 and 13hh), and the
bigger Double Pottock (12.2 to 14.2hh).
• **BREEDING** The Pottock is another Tarpan
descendant and its habitat is the mountainous
Basque region where, for generations, it was
used as a pack pony. Attempts have been
made, with some success, to upgrade the
ponies using Welsh and Arabian blood.
• **CHARACTERISTICS** The Pottock is
hardy and resourceful and is said to be of a
tractable disposition, but has a number of
conformational defects. Interestingly, there
is a slight dish between the
eyes on the otherwise
unremarkable head.

INFLUENCES

ARABIAN
Added quality,
temperament,
and the usual
sound physique.

WELSH B
The source of
bone, substance,
and definite pony
character.

*overloaded
• shoulders*

*straight
• back*

*quarters are not
long, and slope
down from the
croup, but tail is
• carried fairly high*

HEIGHT
Stands between 11 and 14.2hh.

FRANCE: BASQUE REGION

*legs are
generally light
and lack bone*

*hooves are sound
• and strong*

Colors Bay, Brown, Part	Uses Pack, Saddle, Harness

Environment Cool temperate	Origin Pre-Ice Age	Blood Warm

SHETLAND

In comparison to its size, the diminutive pony of the
Shetland Islands is one of the world's most powerful
equines. It is capable of carrying a man over rough country
and is able to work in the fields under heavy loads. It is now
popular and bred extensively all over Europe and in the
Americas and Australasia. It can be ridden by small children,
is excellent in harness, and is still in demand for circus work.

UK: SHETLAND ISLANDS,
SCOTLAND

• **BREEDING** Its original habitat is the bleak Shetland
Islands northeast of Scotland. This inhospitable
environment has governed its character and size. The
ponies arrived in Shetland, probably from Scandinavia,
as long as 10,000 years ago, and may have been
related to primitive Tundra stock. In the 19th
century, Shetlands were used extensively in the
coal mines and a heavier type developed which
has now been largely eradicated. The first
export of 75 ponies was made to Eli Elliot in
America in 1885. Since then, US and
Canadian breeders have produced a new
Shetland pony (see pp.94–95), which bears
little resemblance to the original.
• **CHARACTERISTICS** The Shetland
is naturally hardy and able to thrive in the
harshest environment. It is long-lived,
robust, and sound. The action is quick,
free, and straight, with a characteristic
lift in the knee and hock joints.

*legs have sharply
defined joints and
• strong, flat bone*

*sensible, intelligent •
head with a neat
and sometimes
square muzzle*

Colors All	Uses Saddle, Harness

small, alert ears •

mane and tail are
exceptionally full,
affording protection
against the weather •

nasal cavities are •
large, allowing air
to warm up before
entering the lungs

HEIGHT
Measured in inches,
stands up to 40 in (102 cm).

legs are short •
and strong

round, tough
hooves of hard
blue horn •

INFLUENCE

**TUNDRA
HORSE**
The source of its
tough resistance
to cold and wet.

Environment Cool temperate	Origin Pre-Ice Age	Blood Warm

HIGHLAND

The Highland is a breed of great antiquity. There were
ponies inhabiting northern Scotland and the Scottish islands
following the Ice Age, and some of the horses depicted in
cave drawings at Lascaux, France (15–20,000 years ago)
strongly resemble the modern Highland.
• **BREEDING** In the early 16th century, French horses,
probably predecessors of the Percheron, were crossed with
native stock. Spanish horses were introduced over the
following 200 years. The Dukes of Atholl, foremost among
Highland breeders, used oriental blood, and, in the 19th
century, a Syrian Arabian established the Calgary strain on the
Island of Mull. There was also a strong Clydesdale influence.
• **CHARACTERISTICS** The Highland has exceptional
strength and a docile temperament. It is used in forestry,
in harness, and to carry deer carcasses (weighing
251 lb/114 kg) off the hills when herds are culled. The
Highland is also an active riding pony, much used
for trail riding and mountain packing. The breed is
surefooted, easily kept, free from hereditary
disease, and long-lived.

UK: HIGHLANDS AND
ISLANDS, SCOTLAND

*back is very strong and
usually marked by a
dorsal eel stripe* •

*good hooves, free
• from disease*

INFLUENCES

PONY TYPE 2
Provided the
primitive base;
governed the
initial type.

PERCHERON
Increased size,
combined with
free movement
and refinement.

ARABIAN
Improved quality
and movement;
contributed to
riding action.

CLYDESDALE
Gave more size
and weight, but
also introduced
coarseness.

Colors All, including Dun	Uses Saddle, Pack, Harness

HEIGHT
Stands around 14.2hh.

neck is strong, but does not lack length •

withers are inclined to be low •

head, which has an alert, kindly expression, is short between eyes and muzzle, with a wide forehead • and wide nostrils

conformation is compact, • with depth through the big body and well-sprung ribs

soft, silky • feathering on legs

Environment Moorland	Origin 1st–2nd century AD	Blood Warm

DALES

The powerful Dales pony is a close relation of the Fell pony, both geographically and genetically. However, it is a more heavily built animal and taller than the Fell.

• **BREEDING** The Dales comes from the eastern Pennine area of North Yorkshire, Durham, and Northumberland in England. It was developed as a pack pony in the 18th and 19th centuries to take lead ore from the moorland mines to the seaports. It was also used in coal mines and for farm work. Crosses were made to Welsh Cobs and to the Clydesdale.

• **CHARACTERISTICS** The modern, more refined Dales pony is a brilliant performer in harness, and its calm temperament, sure-footedness, and weight-carrying ability make it a valuable riding pony.

INFLUENCES

FRIESIAN Appearance (including color) and good action were transmitted.

HEIGHT
Stands around 14.2hh.

great propulsive power of hocks is made possible by strong quarters •

• *head is sensible and now shows no trace of Clydesdale influence*

strong shoulders are of harness type and contribute to the raised knee action •

legs are short and powerful with • *silky feathering*

breed is famous for the excellence of its hooves •

UK: EASTERN PENNINES, ENGLAND

Colors Black	Uses Harness, Saddle

Environment Moorland	Origin 1st–2nd century AD	Blood Warm

FELL

The Fell is the modern equivalent of the now extinct Scottish Galloway, a swift, enduring horse which probably formed part of the stock of English "running horses" from which the Thoroughbred racehorse evolved.

• **BREEDING** The native home of the Fell lies in the western Pennines, in Cumbria, England. As with the Dales, it was influenced by the coldblood Friesian horses, used by the Roman legions. The most famous of the Fell lines is Lingcropper, a stallion found on the moors during the Jacobite uprisings of 1745.

• **CHARACTERISTICS** Acknowledged as a harness pony of competition standard and a riding pony of particular ability, the Fell provided a base for the Hackney Pony (see pp.70–71) and is an excellent cross to produce under-saddle competition horses.

INFLUENCES

FRIESIAN Provided sound base stock with excellent bone and substance.

GALLOWAY Added speed, spirit, and sure-footedness to the Fell pony.

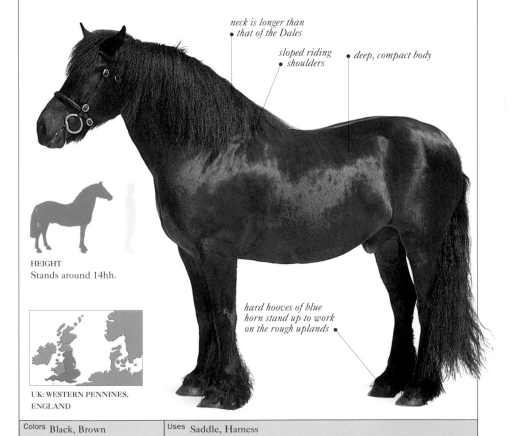

neck is longer than
• that of the Dales

sloped riding
• shoulders

• deep, compact body

HEIGHT
Stands around 14hh.

hard hooves of blue
horn stand up to work
on the rough uplands •

UK: WESTERN PENNINES,
ENGLAND

Colors Black, Brown	Uses Saddle, Harness

Environment Moorland, Stud	Origin 19th century	Blood Warm

HACKNEY PONY

The Hackney Pony shares the studbook with the bigger
Hackney Horse (see pp.154–155) and to a large degree has a
common ancestry in the Norfolk and Yorkshire Trotters of
the 18th and 19th centuries. The Hackney Pony is a real
pony with pony character, not simply a small horse. The
modern Hackney Pony is confined largely to the show ring,
where its spectacular action is an exciting sight.

UK: CUMBRIA, ENGLAND

• **BREEDING** Essentially, the breed was the creation of
Christopher Wilson of Kirkby Lonsdale in Cumbria,
England. By the 1880s, he had created a distinctive type,
based on the local Fell pony with occasional Welsh crosses.
Wilson's champion pony stallion, Sir George, was by a
Yorkshire Trotter and traced his descent through the great
Norfolk Phenomenon to the first notable racehorse,
Flying Childers. Sir George's female progeny were
mated back to their sire to produce elegant ponies
with brilliant harness action. Their height was
limited by being wintered on the fells, where they
were left to fend for themselves, a practice that
ensured a remarkable hardiness of constitution.

• **CHARACTERISTICS** The Hackney Pony
has a naturally brilliant, high-stepping action in
harness. Full of courage, it has great stamina
and is hardy and constitutionally sound. A very
elegant pony, it shows notable quality in the
head, and its coat is particularly fine and silky.

*broad,
strong loins* •

*big, clearly
defined joints
allow maximum
• flexion*

INFLUENCES

FELL
The hardy base
stock descended
from the swift
Galloways.

**NORFOLK
TROTTER**
Gave fast trotting
action and endless
stamina.

WELSH A
Contributed pony
character, along
with quality, spirit,
and movement.

Colors All solid	Uses Harness

HEIGHT
Stands between 12.2
and 14hh.

*characteristic
• pony head*

*no undue
length in
• the back*

*• high neck carriage, low
withers, and powerful
shoulders are ideal for
a harness collar*

*symmetrical •
quarters*

*• compact body with
ample depth through
the chest*

*stands with forelegs
straight and hindlegs
back, to cover
maximum ground •*

*hocks of
notable
strength •*

Environment Moorland	Origin Pre-Ice Age	Blood Warm

EXMOOR

The Exmoor, the oldest of the British mountain and moorland breeds, is probably as old as any equine. It has a number of unique features found in its ancestor, Pony Type 1 (see pp.10–11). These include, for example, a particular jaw formation with a seventh molar, not present in other equines.

• BREEDING This breed belongs on Exmoor in southwest England. Efforts to "improve" the breed have usually had no success, the ponies retaining the character brought about by the isolation and harshness of their home. When they are bred away from Exmoor they soon lose type, and it is necessary to return to moor stock to keep character.

• CHARACTERISTICS Exmoors are strong enough to carry a grown man. Although they have an independent nature, they make magnificent children's ponies and are exceptional jumpers. They are hardy, robust, and sound. Crossed with the Thoroughbred, they produce tough performance horses.

INFLUENCE

PONY TYPE 1 Gave a strong constitution and resistance to the cold and wet.

HEIGHT
Stands between 12.2 and 12.3hh.

"ice" tail has a thick, fanlike growth at the top as weather protection

"toad" eye is hooded

long nasal passages, which allow air to be warmed before inhalation

legs are short and uniformly correct, with good bone

hooves are hard and neat

UK: EXMOOR, SOMERSET, ENGLAND

Colors Bay, Brown, no White	Uses Saddle

Environment Moorland	Origin 12th century	Blood Warm

DARTMOOR

The Dartmoor is the neighbor to the Exmoor. It has been subject to a far greater degree of outside influence than the Exmoor because of the geographical position of its habitat, affording access from the sea and from the route existing between Plymouth and Exeter from early times. Few purebred Dartmoors are found on the moor today. The modern Dartmoor, now an elegant riding pony, is bred at private studs all over Britain, as well as some on the European mainland.

• **BREEDING** The breed originated on the rough moorland of the Dartmoor Forest in Devon, which has had an equine population since ancient times. Oriental blood was introduced as early as the 12th century, and there is a Welsh and Thoroughbred influence. The greatest modern influence was The Leat, a stallion foaled in 1918, by the Arabian, Dwarka.

• **CHARACTERISTICS** The modern Dartmoor is a brilliant riding pony with great jumping ability, and is notable for its long, low action.

HEIGHT
Stands around 12.2hh.

ARABIAN
The upgrading and refining influence on the base stock.

WELSH A
Acted to retain pony character with good bone and substance.

THOROUGHBRED
Gave the breed better scope and much improved the riding action.

• *fine, sloped riding shoulders ensure brilliant movement*

excellent legs and good hooves are the hallmark of the • *Dartmoor*

UK: DARTMOOR, DEVON, ENGLAND

Colors Bay, Brown	Uses Saddle

Environment Moorland	Origin Prehistoric	Blood Warm

NEW FOREST PONY

The New Forest Pony is one of the larger of the native British breeds and one of the most commercially viable because of its versatility. The best of the modern "Foresters" are usually studbred, although the New Forest itself still supports a large number of feral ponies. The latter are owned by the Commoners, who hold traditional grazing rights.

UK: NEW FOREST, ENGLAND

• **BREEDING** Due to the accessibility of the New Forest, through which ran the western routes to Winchester (once England's capital city), the New Forest Pony has very mixed origins. Welsh ponies were used to upgrade stock as early as 1208. Marske, the sire of Eclipse, arguably the greatest racehorse ever, was used briefly around 1765. An Arabian and a Barb stallion were loaned by Queen Victoria in the following century, and Lord Cecil and Lord Lucas brought in Highlands, Fells, Dales, Dartmoors, Exmoors, and more Welsh stock. Despite this broad mix of blood, the New Forest Pony is stamped as a product of its environment.

• **CHARACTERISTICS** The New Forest Pony is an excellent all-arounder. Big enough to carry adults, it has exceptional riding shoulders and a long, low action that is particularly marked at the canter. The ponies are easy to handle and friendly.

pleasantly symmetrical quarters, indicative of potential speed •

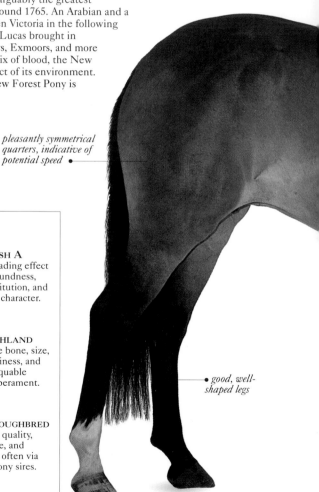

• good, well-shaped legs

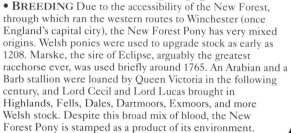

INFLUENCES

WELSH A
Upgrading effect on soundness, constitution, and pony character.

HIGHLAND
Gave bone, size, hardiness, and an equable temperament.

THOROUGHBRED
Added quality, courage, and action, often via polo pony sires.

Colors All solid	Uses Saddle, Harness

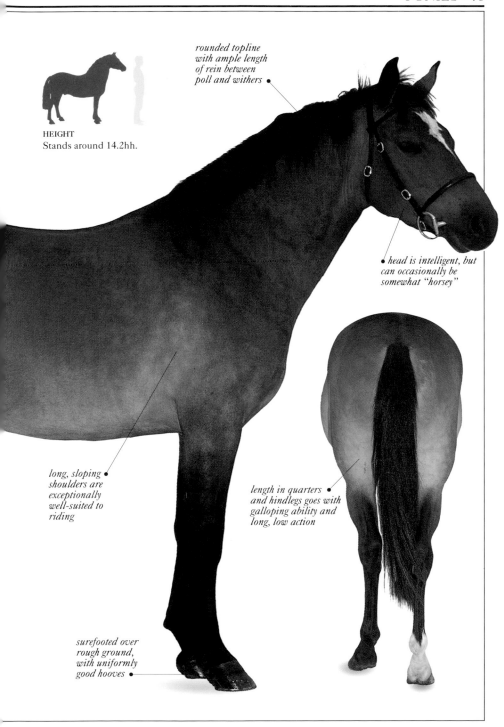

rounded topline
with ample length
of rein between
poll and withers •

HEIGHT
Stands around 14.2hh.

• head is intelligent, but
can occasionally be
somewhat "horsey"

long, sloping •
shoulders are
exceptionally
well-suited to
riding

length in quarters •
and hindlegs goes with
galloping ability and
long, low action

surefooted over
rough ground,
with uniformly
good hooves •

Environment Moorland	Origin 15th–16th century	Blood Warm

CONNEMARA

The Connemara, which originated on Ireland's western seaboard, is that country's sole indigenous pony. It is now bred throughout Europe, as well as further afield. Of all the mountain and moorland breeds, it is probably the most commercially viable because it is fast, a brilliant performance pony, and a superb jumper, while being big enough to be ridden by older children and lightweight adults.

IRELAND: CONNEMARA

• **BREEDING** Barb and Spanish horses were introduced to the indigenous stock early. The result was the renowned fast, agile, and hardy Irish Hobby of the 16th and 17th centuries. In the 19th century, government efforts, aimed at checking degeneration in the native stock, used Arabians, Welsh Cobs, Roadsters, and Thoroughbreds. Later, Irish Drafts were also used. The first stallion in the studbook was Cannon Ball, grandson of the Welsh Cob, Prince Llewellyn. More recent lines are Carna Dun by the Thoroughbred, Little Heaven, and Clonkeehan Auratum by the Arabian Naseel.

• **CHARACTERISTICS** The Connemara has emerged as a fixed type, retaining the hardiness inherited from its environment. Crosses to the Thoroughbred produce excellent competition horses with much pony hardiness and sense.

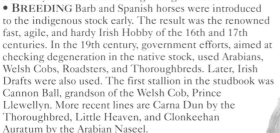

• *distinctive head is invariably fine and neat, never becoming heavy, and reveals Arabian and Thoroughbred blood*

• *length from hips to hocks contributes to speed and jumping ability*

Colors All solid, including Dun	Uses Saddle

HEIGHT
Stands between 13 and 14.2hh.

*length of rein is
• exceptional*

• *excellent sloping
shoulders of a
pronounced riding type*

*bone measurement is •
often a surprising
7–8 in (18–20 cm)*

INFLUENCES

SPANISH
Passed on Barb
qualities as well
as Sorraia vigor
and hardiness.

WELSH D
The source of the
breed's robust
constitution and
marked strength.

THOROUGHBRED
Transmitted its
scope, courage,
speed, and
improved action.

Environment Mountain, Moor	Origin Prehistoric	Blood Warm

WELSH MOUNTAIN PONY

The Welsh Mountain Pony (Section A in the Welsh Pony and Cob Society studbook, opened in 1902) is probably the most numerous of the British mountain and moorland breeds. It is the base from which the Welsh Pony (Section B) and the two divisions of Welsh Cobs (Sections C and D) evolved.

• **BREEDING** Indigenous ponies populated the Welsh hills long before the Roman occupation of Britain. The Romans introduced eastern blood, and eastern influence continued until the birth of the breed's patriarch, Dyoll Starlight, in 1894.

• **CHARACTERISTICS** The Welsh Mountain Pony is recognized as being the most beautiful of the pony breeds. As well as this beauty, it retains all the hardiness and hereditary soundness derived from its early environment on the wild Welsh uplands.

INFLUENCES

ARABIAN
Gave quality, kind temperament, and sound physique and constitution.

BARB
Transmitted fire, toughness, powers of endurance, and marked stamina.

THOROUGHBRED
Noted for its speed and courage, its presence improved scope and action.

• *beautiful head clearly reveals powerful eastern influence*

HEIGHT
Stands around 12hh.

UK: WALES

• *body is notably compact, with great depth through the girth*

Colors All solid	Uses Saddle, Harness

Environment Mountain, Moor	Origin Prehistoric	Blood Warm

WELSH PONY

The Welsh Pony (Section B) is described as a riding pony that retains the character and temperament of the Welsh Mountain Pony.

• **BREEDING** Early Section B ponies were often the result of crossings between small Welsh Cobs and Welsh Mountain Ponies. The foundation of the modern pony is attributed to Tan-y-Bwlch Berwyn, foaled in 1924, by the Arabian (or Barb) stallion Sahara. Berwyn's son, Berwynfa, founded the Coed Coch Section B herd. Other notable lines have descended from the Arabian sires, Skowronek and Raseem.

• **CHARACTERISTICS** The Section B pony is an elegant, quality pony. More versatile than the Mountain Pony because of its larger size, it excels in competitive disciplines and jumps well. Its action is longer and lower than that of the Mountain Pony.

INFLUENCES

ARABIAN
Gave quality, kind temperament, and sound physique and constitution.

BARB
Transmitted fire, toughness, powers of endurance, and marked stamina.

THOROUGHBRED
Noted for its speed and courage, its presence improved scope and action.

HEIGHT
Stands around 13.2hh.

UK: WALES

• *excellent depth of girth, sometimes called "Welsh breadbasket"*

noticeably longer • proportions than those of the Welsh Mountain Pony

Colors All solid	Uses Saddle, Harness

Environment Mountain, Moor	Origin 12th century	Blood Warm

WELSH PONY OF COB TYPE

The smaller of the two Welsh Cobs is that belonging to
Section C in the studbook, where it is referred to as "the
Welsh Pony of Cob Type." These small cobs were often
called "farm ponies." They were used for every sort of
work on the Welsh hill farms, as well as being employed
extensively in the North Wales coal mines during the 19th
century. After World War II, when the type seemed in danger
of disappearing, a new section (Section C) was opened in the
studbook to preserve this essentially Welsh working pony.
Today, the Section C ponies are still used very successfully
in harness, as they were in the past. They are also an
excellent choice for packing and trail riding. Naturally
courageous and good jumpers, they make wonderful hunting
ponies for young people and light adults.

• **BREEDING** In the early days, the cob-type pony was
usually the progeny of a Welsh Mountain mare and a small
cob stallion. The stallions were, in effect, slightly larger,
heavier, and more thickset versions of the Welsh
Mountain Pony. In recent years, the most significant
Section C stallions have had a strong background
of Mountain Pony, their sires being Section A
stallions, like the prolific and very successful Coed
Coch Madog, the sire of both Lyn Cwmcoed and
Synod William. Increasingly, however, the
Welsh Pony of Cob Type is being produced
by the mating of parents, both of whom are
registered in Section C of the studbook.

• **CHARACTERISTICS** The Section C Cob
has all the attributes of the Welsh Mountain
Pony. It is tough, hardy, constitutionally
sound, and has wonderfully made legs and
hooves. Able to live outside all year, it is easy
to manage and economical to keep.

UK: WALES

*overall outline
is compact and
indicative of strength* •

INFLUENCES

WELSH A
Imparted the
essential Welsh
character to the
Welsh Section C.

WELSH COB
Responsible for
the increase in
size required in
the "farm pony."

Colors All solid	Uses Saddle, Harness

HEIGHT
Stands around 13.2hh.

• thickset neck,
carried high
and arched

arresting head
reflects the Welsh
• Mountain Pony

despite low withers, •
shoulders are long
and action is strong
and vigorous

strong legs may •
have fine, silky
feathering at heels

hooves are strong
with hard horn •

Environment Cool temperate	Origin Pre-Ice Age	Blood Warm

BARDIGIANO

Outside of Britain, there are few European pony breeds of note in the modern context. Italy's Bardigiano, although little known and not enjoying the benefit of a "closed" studbook, is a possible exception, along with the obscure Asturçon pony, which exists in very small numbers in the mountainous regions of northern Spain.

• **BREEDING** The Bardigiano is a mountain breed from the northern Appenine region of Italy. Like the Asturçon, it resembles to a degree the oldest of the British native ponies, the Exmoor, and there is probably some common Celtic pony root stock. It is generally accepted, however, that the Bardigiano, while owing something to the heavier Italian mountain strains, has a pronounced connection with the Avelignese, an Italian breed that is related to the Haflinger. Indeed, the Avelignese has the same ancestors as the latter, and both descend from the extinct Avellinum-Haflinger. The Arabian El Bedavi was the recognized founding stallion of the Haflinger and had considerable influence on the Avelignese. The oriental influence is apparent in the Bardigiano.

• **CHARACTERISTICS** This is a strong, well-made pony of considerable character. It is hardy, quick-moving, surefooted, and ideally suited to any kind of mountain work.

ITALY: NORTHERN
APPENINE REGION

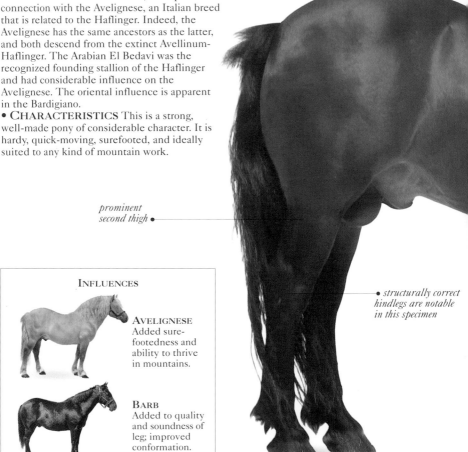

prominent second thigh •

• *structurally correct hindlegs are notable in this specimen*

INFLUENCES

AVELIGNESE
Added sure-footedness and ability to thrive in mountains.

BARB
Added to quality and soundness of leg; improved conformation.

Colors All solid	Uses Pack, Light Draft

HEIGHT
Stands between 12 and 13hh.

characteristic short,
pricked ears

forehand is remarkable
for its obvious strength

shoulders are inclined
to be upright

a real pony head,
neat and tapering
prettily to the
muzzle

body is short,
compact, and has a
well-sprung ribcage

Environment Hot temperate	Origin Pre-Ice Age	Blood Warm

SORRAIA

The first horses to be domesticated in Europe are thought
to be those of the Iberian Peninsula. Today, descendants
of those early equines, the "primitive" founding races, are
still found in both Spain and Portugal. Among these are
the Sorraia, in some specimens still bearing a remarkable
resemblance in color and conformation to the Tarpan, and
the more refined Garrano or Minho, of the same root stock,
with a habitat further to the north in the mountain valleys
of Garrano do Minho and Traz dos Montes.

PORTUGAL: PLAINS OF SOR
AND RAIA

• **BREEDING** The Sorraia lived in the plains between
the rivers Sor and Raia, and for some years the famous
d'Andrade family kept a small herd in its natural state.
It has to be assumed that this native base stock, once
it had been subjected to the powerful North African
Barb influence, contributed to the renowned
Spanish horse, and via that pervasive blood to
a variety of different breeds.

• **CHARACTERISTICS** For centuries, the
Sorraia was used by local cowboys and for light
agricultural work and, in times past, it could
hardly have been considered a prepossessing
specimen. Nonetheless, for all its heavy head
and low-set tail, it retained all the primitive
vigor of its wild ancestors.

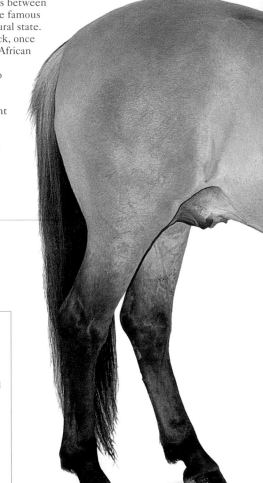

*low-set, usually •
black tail*

INFLUENCES

TARPAN
Primitive root
stock provided
constitutional
soundness.

BARB
Improved move-
ment, increased
size, and added
fiery character.

Colors Gray-dun	Uses Feral, Light Agricultural

length of rein is
a notable feature

HEIGHT
Stands between 12.2
and 13hh.

short, powerful neck is
reminiscent of the Spanish and
Portuguese breeds

black-tipped ears, set high on
the head, are typical, as are
a black mane and tail

body is compact and
of exceptional depth in
this example of the
"improved" Sorraia

Environment Mediterranean	Origin Pre–Ice Age	Blood Warm

SKYRIAN HORSE

Skyros, in the Aegean Sea, has supported ponies since ancient times. The ponies lived in the mountains and were brought down to help with the wheat threshing. The modern pony, called the Skyrian Horse by its breeders, has a utilitarian role, but is also used for riding.
• **BREEDING** The proportions of the Skyrian incline toward those of a horse, and it resembles horses depicted in the statuary and friezes of Ancient Greece. It is possible there is a connection with the Thessalanian horse, which would point toward Horse Type 4 as an origin, although the coat pattern shows there may be a relationship to the Tarpan.
• **CHARACTERISTICS** The Skyrian is tough, hardy, good-tempered, and willing. In relation to its size, it jumps well. It is straight in the shoulders, usually cow-hocked, and mean in the quarters. The coat is often marked with an eel stripe and zebra bars. The feet are always black, a breed society requirement.

INFLUENCE

HORSE TYPE 4
Prototype Arabian; transmitted some conformational quality.

neat head with small, pointed ears •

narrow, sloping croup, with quarters lacking • in muscle

narrow body with generally upright shoulders •

HEIGHT
Stands around 11hh.

GREECE: ISLAND OF SKYROS

Colors Bay, Dun	Uses Saddle, Harness, Pack

Environment Mountain	Origin Pre–Ice Age	Blood Warm

PINDOS PONY

The Pindos Pony, larger than the Skyrian, comes from the mountainous areas of Thessaly and Epirus, the traditional horse lands of Ancient Greece. It is used as a surefooted pack pony, in agricultural pursuits and forestry, and as a riding and driving pony. Pindos mares are often used for breeding mules.

• **BREEDING** The Pindos, in all probability, descends directly from the Thessalanian. Over the centuries, it is also likely to have been influenced by the ancient Peloponnese, Arcadian, and Epidaurian breeds.

• **CHARACTERISTICS** The Pindos Pony is tough, enduring, and can survive on minimal forage. The tail is set high (indicating Horse Type 4 in its ancestry), but the quarters are poor, with little second thigh. The hooves are hard, narrow, and boxy, and are rarely, if ever, shod. The Pindos is noted for its stamina but has the reputation of being very stubborn.

INFLUENCE

HORSE TYPE 4 Prototype Arabian; transmitted some conformational quality.

head is inclined to be long, but shows a certain quality

back is strong in comparison to quarters; shoulders less upright than might be expected

cannons are long, and deficient in bone

hooves are very hard

HEIGHT
Stands around 13hh.

GREECE : THESSALONIKA

Colors Bay, Black, Brown	Uses Saddle, Harness, Pack

Environment Desert	Origin Prehistoric	Blood Hot

CASPIAN

The Caspian pony, in fact a miniature horse, may be the most ancient breed in existence and could, it is suggested, be the ancestor of the Arabian. Caspians were "discovered" by Mrs. Louise L. Firouz at Amol on the Caspian littoral, Iran, in 1965 and there are now Caspian societies in Britain, Australia, New Zealand, and the USA.

• **BREEDING** The breed appears to be the direct descendant of Horse Type 4 (see pp.14–15), described as the prototype Arabian, which had its habitat in western Asia. Egyptian and Persian artifacts of the pre-Christian era (from 1,200–500 BC) depict similar small horses of great refinement.

• **CHARACTERISTICS** The Caspian differs in physical character from other equines. For instance, there is a difference in the shape of the scapula and the formation of the parietal bones of the head. Although small, the Caspian is fast enough to keep up with much larger horses, and it is also an exceptional jumper.

MIDDLE EAST: ARABIAN PENINSULA

• *body is narrow and light, with the proportions and length that are associated with speed*

hooves are small, oval-shaped, very hard and strong, and not subject to disease •

Colors Bay, Chestnut	Uses Saddle, Harness

ears are not
longer than
4½ in (11.5 cm)

long, arched neck

withers are
relatively high
and sharp

head is short
and covered in
fine, thin skin

shoulders are
formed like those of a
horse and produce a
long, low stride

body, although deep,
is narrow in build and
thus very suitable for
young riders

HEIGHT
Stands between 10 and 12hh.

slim legs, with little or
no feathering, are said
to have dense bone

INFLUENCE

HORSE TYPE 4
As the prototype,
this horse passed
on many Arabian
traits.

Environment Steppe, Savanna	Origin Pre-Ice Age	Blood Warm

BASHKIR

The Bashkir of the Russian steppe is an enormously tough pony. It is bred under state supervision as a pack, draft, and saddle animal, as well as for meat and milk. A mare may give up to 350 gallons (1,600 liters) during a lactation period which lasts seven to eight months. There are about 1,000 Bashkirs (called "Bashkir Curly" because of the curly coat) in the United States. They are reputed to have been popular with the native Americans of the northwestern states.

NORTHERN EURASIA:
RUSSIAN FEDERATION

• **BREEDING** The Bashkir, or Bashkirsky, evolved centuries ago around the southern foothills of the Urals in Bashkiria. Two types of Bashkir have since developed in the Russian Federation: a mountain pony and a steppe pony, the latter being more predominantly of harness type.
• **CHARACTERISTICS** Bashkirs are kept outside in herds, often in subzero temperatures, and are able to fend for themselves and find food in deep snow. This predominantly chestnut-colored pony grows a thick, curly winter coat, which can be spun to make cloth. Among the hardiest breeds, it can work hard without supplementary feed. A pair of Bashkirs is reputed to be able to pull a sleigh 75–87 miles (120–140 km) in 24 hours, without being fed.

HEIGHT
Stands around 14hh.

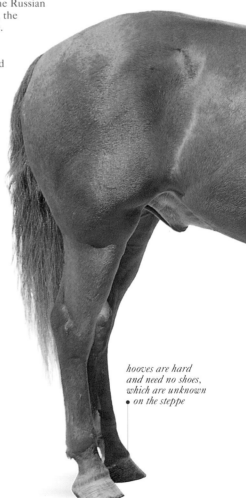

hooves are hard and need no shoes, which are unknown • on the steppe

---

INFLUENCES

TARPAN
A primitive influence which gave added freedom of action.

PRZEWALSKI'S HORSE
The dominant primitive gene; gave stamina.

Colors Chestnut, Bay	Uses Pack, Draft

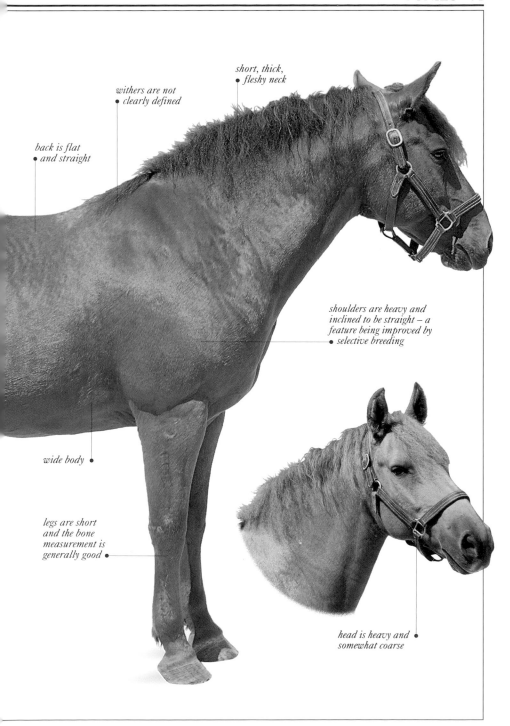

short, thick,
• fleshy neck

withers are not
• clearly defined

back is flat
• and straight

shoulders are heavy and
inclined to be straight – a
feature being improved by
• selective breeding

wide body •

legs are short
and the bone
measurement is
generally good •

head is heavy and •
somewhat coarse

Environment Temperate grassland	Origin 20th century	Blood Warm

AUSTRALIAN PONY

The Australian Pony is now a breed in its own right. It is controlled by the Australian Pony Studbook Society, a body formed in 1929 to produce children's riding ponies. The Association lays down a detailed standard of conformation.

• **BREEDING** The Australian Pony has evolved from an assortment of equine breeds and types, imported initially by the early settlers. The first pony import to arrive in Australia was in 1803, but by 1920 a pony of distinctive type had been established. Welsh Mountain Ponies provided much of the breeding stock, along with Shetland blood, as well as that of the Hackney, and also infusions of Arabian and Thoroughbred.

• **CHARACTERISTICS** The Australian pony resembles the Welsh Mountain Pony more closely than any other breed. It is compact, well-built, and strong, and is essentially a quality pony of correct conformation and very good free action. There is a pronounced pony character, very evident in the neat, refined head and the large eyes. It is considered to have the best of temperaments and has more in common with the British native ponies than with the specialized riding pony.

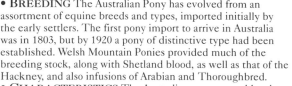

AUSTRALIA

quarters are generous and well-shaped •

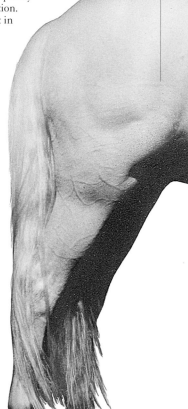

INFLUENCES

WELSH A
A dominant influence that contributed to pony character.

SHETLAND
Gave inherent hardiness and constitutional strength.

THOROUGHBRED
Improved action; provided extra scope and jumping ability.

HACKNEY
Added to brilliance of action; gave a particular spirit.

Colors All solid	Uses Saddle

topline is nicely
rounded, with
an attractively
curved neck •

HEIGHT
Stands between 12 and 14hh.

• forehand is notable
for the excellent slope
of the shoulder

overall impression of
refinement derives
• from the Welsh Pony

• overall outline is
reminiscent of the
Welsh Pony, the
major influence

• profile is slightly
concave, with big,
widely spaced eyes and
a neat, tapered muzzle

Environment Temperate, Controlled	Origin 20th century	Blood Warm

AMERICAN SHETLAND

The American Shetland is the most popular pony in North America. The first import from the Shetland Islands, off the coast of Scotland, was made in 1885. An American Shetland Pony Club was formed in 1888, but the American Shetland is an invented breed, bearing no resemblance to the distinctive, hardy Island pony.

• **BREEDING** America's modern Shetland was created by crossing finer-built examples of the Island pony with Hackney Ponies, the subsequent progeny being given a particular character by further crossings to small Arabians and Thoroughbreds. Although the ponies do not retain the pure Shetland's legendary native hardiness and constitution, they are versatile. Primarily a show harness pony, it also races in harness, and those termed hunter-types are shown and jumped under saddle.

• **CHARACTERISTICS** The intelligent and good-natured American Shetland resembles the Hackney in outline and conformation. Narrower than the true Shetland Pony, it has greater length in the proportions. Although the relatively long head lacks pony character, the impression is of considerable refinement.

USA

broad, strong loins

hair of tail and mane is long and thick

stance is stretched and typical of the harness pony

Colors All solid	Uses Harness

set of neck resembles
that of the Hackney •

• relatively
long ears

HEIGHT
Stands up to 11.2hh.

long head and •
straight profile
show little pony
character

• frame is long and
narrow in relation
to overall size

INFLUENCES

HACKNEY
Imparted its
spirit and
spectacular
trotting action.

characteristic long,
slim legs, with
some tendency to
long cannons •

SHETLAND
The base stock
ensured small
stature and
soundness.

Environment Cool temperate	Origin 20th century	Blood Warm

ROCKY MOUNTAIN PONY

The American Rocky Mountain Pony is probably the latest
addition to the world's horse population. The registry was
opened as recently as 1986, but since then there has been a
steady development of this distinctive and attractive animal.
Further recognition of the Rocky Mountain Pony has been
given by the inclusion of a good specimen in the Breeds'
Barn at the Kentucky Horse Park in Lexington, Kentucky.

USA: ROCKY MOUNTAINS

• **BREEDING** Visually, it is not difficult to see the connection
between the Rocky Mountain Pony and the Spanish imports
of early American history. However, credit for the development
of the Rocky Mountain belongs to Sam Tuttle of Stout Springs,
Kentucky, who held the riding concession at Natural Bridge
State Park. Tuttle's stallion, Old Tobe, was a favorite with
the riders because of his smooth and surefooted lateral
gait (the amble or pace). He was a prepotent, prolific
sire who became the patriarch of a distinctive
group of horses that inherited his
conformation, action, and temperament.

• **CHARACTERISTICS** The gait and the unusual
coloring are the principal features of the Rocky
Mountain Pony. It ambles smoothly on rough
ground at about 7 mph (11 km/h), and can reach
speeds of 16 mph (25 km/h) for shorter distances
on the flat. The most prized coat coloring is the
unusual rich chocolate shade accompanied by a
flaxen mane and tail. The breed is hardy and
able to tolerate severe mountain winters.

*full, flaxen tail
complements the rich
chocolate coat* •

HEIGHT
Stands between 14.2
and 15hh.

*pony is very
surefooted
and hooves
are hard
• and strong*

INFLUENCE

SPANISH
The influence
is evident in
the gait, color,
and outline.

Colors Chocolate	Uses Saddle

neck is long and
graceful, contributing
to good balance •

back curves nicely
• up to the croup

withers are fairly
low and flat •

shoulders are not built for
galloping, but are strong
and well-placed in relation
• to the neck

body, although •
unexceptional, is
pleasingly rounded
in proportion to the
overall structure

head is handsome, •
with large ears

Environment Cool temperate	Origin 16th century	Blood Warm

CHINCOTEAGUE/ASSATEAGUE

Ponies living in the islands of Chincoteague
and Assateague, off the coast of Virginia, are
some of the last wild stock in the world. Most
of the 200 or so ponies live on Assateague, a
national park, separated from the mainland by
dramatic storms in 1933. Each year the
Assateague ponies are rounded up and swum
over the channel to Chincoteague, where the
young stock are sold. The profits are used to
manage the wild herds.
• **BREEDING** The ponies derive from stock
that strayed or were abandoned in early
colonial times, and which originated from the
Spanish and North African imports. One story
suggests that a ship carrying Barb horses from
North Africa to Peru was wrecked, the horses
swam ashore, and they have lived there ever
since. But there is no evidence to support this.
• **CHARACTERISTICS** Although the ponies
were improved by Pinto, Shetland, and Welsh
pony blood, they would be regarded in
European terms as degenerate in character,
exhibiting the failings of scrub stock.

INFLUENCES

SPANISH
Its inherent
qualities were
diluted by the
harsh habitat.

*withers are inclined
to be lumpy and
shoulders heavy*

*short,
compact body*

*usually light
feather on heels*

HEIGHT
Stands around 12hh.

USA: CHINCOTEAGUE AND
ASSATEAGUE, VIRGINIA

Colors All	Uses Feral, Saddle

Environment Cool temperate	Origin 16th century	Blood Warm

SABLE ISLAND

Sable Island off Nova Scotia, Canada, is a
barren land, resembling a sandbank. For some
400 years it has supported herds of semiwild
ponies, which are named after the island.

• **BREEDING** The present stock originated in
French horses believed to be of predominantly
Norman ancestry, which were probably brought
to the island by a Bostonian Huguenot in 1739.

• **CHARACTERISTICS** Although the ponies
are hardy and tough, their conformation is only
moderate. The
head is large, and
the quarters are
usually weak. The
ponies are said
to be docile and
easily managed
if they are trained
while still young.

INFLUENCE

NORMAN
Influenced the
overall size and
character of this
semiwild breed.

CANADA: SABLE ISLAND,
OFF NOVA SCOTIA

HEIGHT
Stands between 14
and 15hh.

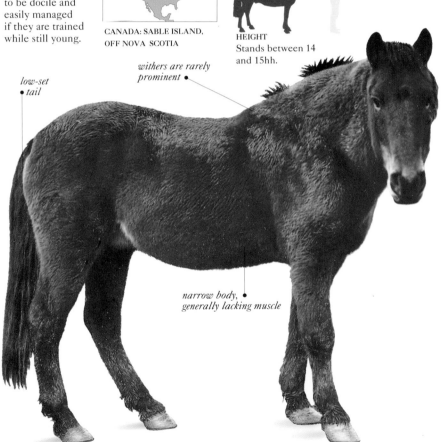

*low-set
• tail*

*withers are rarely
prominent •*

*narrow body, •
generally lacking muscle*

Colors Most solid	Uses Feral, Saddle

Environment Desert, Savanna	Origin 16th century	Blood Warm

GALICENO

The Galiceno pony of Mexico is another example of the
Spanish legacy in the Americas. Since the 1950s, the
Galiceno has spread northward into the USA, being
officially recognized as a breed in 1958. It is regarded as an
ideal "in-between" mount for young riders who are making
the transition from ponies to horses.

MEXICO

• **BREEDING** The Galiceno originated in Galicia in northwest Spain and takes its name from that area. Throughout
Europe, from the earliest times, Galicia was famed for its
smooth gaited horses. The modern Galiceno is still
distinguished by the swift running walk that was so much
prized in Elizabethan England. The ancestors of these
small horses would have been among those brought by the
Spaniards from the West Indies in the 16th century, and
those horses, in turn, are likely to have been descendants of
the indigenous Sorraias and Garranos (the same equine
under different names) of the Iberian Peninsula.

• **CHARACTERISTICS** The tough and hardy
Galiceno is said to be tractable, intelligent, and
versatile. The pony's natural agility and speed
ensure its popularity as a ranch and competition
pony. It is also used in harness and as an
everyday means of transport.

fine head has
a distinctive
• character

• intelligent eyes
are large and
widely spaced

Colors All solid	Uses Saddle, Harness

although narrow and
lightly built, the body is
compact, without too
• much length in the back

• juncture between
head and neck is
graceful, without
thickness in the jowl

• forehand has a
peculiarly shallow chest,
and shoulders that are
inclined to be upright

hard, sound legs •

HEIGHT
Stands around 14hh.

hooves are open,
without a hint
of contraction
at the heel •

INFLUENCE

SPANISH
Contributed to
the appearance,
the constitution,
and the spirit.

Environment Temperate, Controlled	Origin 20th century	Blood Warm

FALABELLA

The natural reasons for small stature in equines are environmental – severe climatic conditions combined with low feed availability. However, it is possible to breed miniatures or, conversely, very large horses deliberately. Miniature horses have been bred as pets and for their curiosity value throughout history. Today, the best-known example is the Falabella, claimed to be a miniature horse, rather than a pony, on account of its proportions and character.

ARGENTINA: BUENOS AIRES

• **BREEDING** The Falabella takes its name from the Falabella family, who developed the breed at the Recreo de Roca Ranch, outside Buenos Aires, Argentina. They crossed the smallest Shetlands with a very small Thoroughbred, thereafter deliberately breeding down by crossing the smallest animals and practicing close inbreeding. The aim was to produce a near-perfect equine specimen in miniature, but inbreeding often results in conformational weaknesses and a loss of vigor. It is said that Falabellas can be used in harness, but they are considered unsuitable for riding. One of the smallest miniatures bred was a mare called Sugar Dumpling, belonging to Smith McCoy of Roderfield, West Virginia. She weighed 30 lb (13.6 kg) and was only 20 in (51 cm) high.

quarters have a tendency to drop away, • with tail set low

• **CHARACTERISTICS** Conformational defects, such as weak hocks, crooked legs, and heavy heads, are fairly common in miniature stock. The best, however, exhibit many of the qualities of a good Shetland. As pets, Falabellas are said to be friendly and intelligent, and some attractive coat colors occur in the breed, including spot patterns.

hocks are sometimes • weak and crooked

HEIGHT
Stands up to 7hh.

INFLUENCE

SHETLAND
The base was small Shetlands, crossed with very small Thoroughbreds.

Colors All, including spotted	Uses Novelty

thick, luxuriant
mane

there is a tendency
to ewe-necks, with
development on
underside

withers are
usually flat

head is often heavy
and large compared
with body

tail, like that of the
Shetland, is thick
and luxuriant

legs may lack
bone and may not
be well-formed

cannons may be
offset from knee
and hock

HORSES

Environment Cool temperate	Origin 19th century	Blood Warm

DØLE GUDBRANDSDAL

Comprising nearly half of the Norwegian horse population, the
Døle Gudbrandsdal resembles British Dales and Fell ponies. All
three derive from the same prehistoric wild stock.

• **BREEDING** Bred in the great central valley of Gudbrandsdal,
Norway, the horses were used in pack and in agriculture. The
breed is noted for its speed at the trot and, although the heavier,
draft type was retained, a lighter Døle Trotter was developed for
harness racing. The Thoroughbred stallion Odin, imported in
1834, had the most significant influence on the Trotter.
State breeding centers were established in 1962, and the
stallions are performance-tested over 1,094 yd (1,000 m)
with a three-minute time limit.

• **CHARACTERISTICS** The Døle Gudbrandsdal is
hardy, and very powerful in relation to its size.

NORWAY: GUDBRANDSDAL
VALLEY

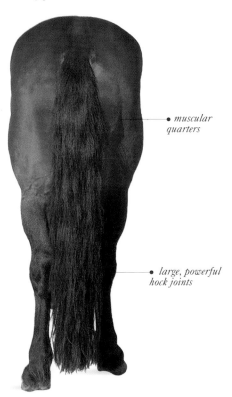

• *muscular
quarters*

• *large, powerful
hock joints*

Colors Black, Brown	Uses Light Draft

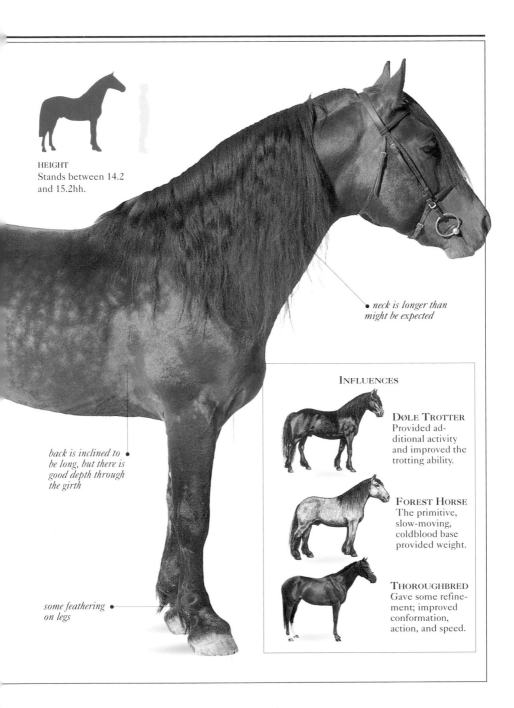

HEIGHT
Stands between 14.2
and 15.2hh.

*neck is longer than
might be expected*

*back is inclined to
be long, but there is
good depth through
the girth*

*some feathering
on legs*

INFLUENCES

DØLE TROTTER
Provided ad-
ditional activity
and improved the
trotting ability.

FOREST HORSE
The primitive,
slow-moving,
coldblood base
provided weight.

THOROUGHBRED
Gave some refine-
ment; improved
conformation,
action, and speed.

Environment Taiga	Origin Pre-Ice Age	Blood Cold

FINNISH HORSE

In times past there were two Finnish breeds, the Finnish Draft and the Finnish Universal, both of which were bred for performance rather than for their appearance. The Draft horse, the heavier of the two, was a sturdy, powerfully built animal, fairly common in its appearance but with quick, active paces. The lighter Universal was a general-purpose animal which could be ridden, used for light transport and, importantly, for harness racing. Since the 1970s, emphasis has shifted toward the lighter utility horse, although there is still a need for horses in agriculture and in the forest industry.

FINLAND

• **BREEDING** The Finnish Horse is probably a descendant of the ancient breeds of both heavy and light horses in Europe, crossed with both cold- and warmblood breeds. A studbook was opened in 1907 for both the heavier and lighter types, and rigorous performance testing was instituted.

• **CHARACTERISTICS** The even-tempered Finnish Horse, despite its relatively small frame, has the draft power of a heavy horse combined with the speed, character, and agility of the light horse breeds. It is long-lived, very enduring, and possessed of remarkable stamina. Needless to say, the breed is noted for its excellent constitution. The slope of the quarters from the croup, combined with some length in the body, is characteristic of the harness racing horse, and is a reflection of the shift in emphasis in the breeding of the Finnish Horse.

slope of the quarters from the croup is characteristic of the • harness racing horse

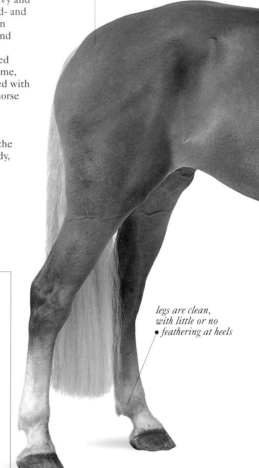

legs are clean, with little or no • feathering at heels

INFLUENCES

FINNISH PONY
Native ponies provided a hardy, enduring base for crosses.

OLDENBURG
Fixed the character and gave additional size and action.

Colors All	Uses Light Draft

HEIGHT
Stands around 15.2hh.

outline is characterized
by a straight, harness-
• type back

shoulders are strong and
more suited to harness
• work than to riding

legs are
uniformly
correct •

• head is inclined to
plainness, but is otherwise
honest and workmanlike,
reflecting the breed's
pleasant disposition

Environment Temperate, Controlled	Origin 17th century	Blood Warm

SWEDISH WARMBLOOD

The Swedish Warmblood was bred originally as a cavalry horse of above average quality. More recently, breeders have concentrated on producing competition horses, capable of performing internationally in the three principal mounted disciplines – jumping, dressage, and eventing.

• **BREEDING** The breed descends from Spanish, oriental, and Friesian stallions imported some 300 years ago, and is the result of carefully supervised breeding policies. The crossing of these horses with local stock at the great studs of Stromsholm (founded 1621) and Flyinge (founded 1658) provided a base for the use of Trakehners, Hanoverians, Arabians, and Thoroughbreds. Stock is rigorously tested and exports are worldwide.

• **CHARACTERISTICS** The Swedish Warmblood is a big, imposing horse. It is sound, of good conformation, and has a sensible temperament, which makes it particularly suitable for dressage. It is also in demand for jumping, eventing, and driving.

SWEDEN

• *short, strong legs*

• *sound hooves*

INFLUENCES

THOROUGHBRED
Used to impart courage, mental stamina, speed, and scope.

ARABIAN
Gave hereditary soundness, spirit, and kindness of temperament.

TRAKEHNER
Provided strength, athletic talent, and stability of temperament.

HANOVERIAN
Added size and strength, an easy disposition, and jumping ability.

Colors All solid	Uses Saddle

HEIGHT
Stands around 16.2hh.

strong shoulders allow
good movement

compact body
with a deep enough
girth and well-
sprung ribs

good
joints

head is pleasant
and "hunterlike,"
with a sensible
expression

Environment Cool temperate	Origin 16th century	Blood Warm

FREDERIKSBORG

DENMARK

In the 16th century, Denmark was a principal source for elegant, active saddle horses and quality military chargers. These horses, called Frederiksborgs, were the product of a stud founded by King Frederik II in 1562. Pluto, a white horse and founder of the Lipizzaner line that carries his name, was a Frederiksborg, foaled at the Royal Danish Court Stud in 1765.

• **BREEDING** The Frederiksborg was founded on Spanish and later related Neapolitan stock. In the 19th century, crosses were made to eastern stallions and halfbreed English stallions. The result was an impressive, lively, riding horse with vigorous action. The breed was also used extensively to improve other stock, including the Jutland (see pp.216–217). Heavy exportation seriously depleted the old stock and, in 1839, the Stud turned to producing Thoroughbred-type animals and the original breed almost disappeared. For a while, private individuals continued to raise Frederiksborgs as smart carriage horses but, as the demand for riding horses grew, Thoroughbreds were used increasingly. It is unlikely that many of the old-type Frederiksborgs survive.

• **CHARACTERISTICS** Although a riding horse, the Frederiksborg always retained a high carriage action described as being "strong and sweeping."

joints are usually • acceptable

• head has an intelligent expression but is otherwise plain and plebeian

Colors Chestnut	Uses Saddle

neck is short and
upright, and
characteristic of the
carriage horse •

withers are flat, and
overall the whole
forehand is suited
to use in harness •

front is short and
shoulders are upright,
which results in a
• strong, high action

body is relatively •
long and girth is
acceptable, but horse
is "on the leg"

HEIGHT
Stands around 15.3hh.

hooves are strong
and well-shaped •

INFLUENCE

SPANISH
The source of
great elegance,
showy action, and
imposing presence.

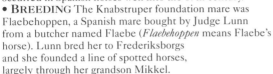

Environment Cool temperate	Origin 19th century	Blood Warm

KNABSTRUPER

Spotted coat patterns were evident in the cave drawings
of Cro-Magnon man 30,000 years ago, and such horses were
frequently much revered in the ancient world. Denmark's
Knabstruper, however, is of more recent origin, the breed
being founded on a Spanish mare in 1808. Spotted strains
occurred in Spanish horses well into the 19th century.
• **BREEDING** The Knabstruper foundation mare was
Flaebehoppen, a Spanish mare bought by Judge Lunn
from a butcher named Flaebe (*Flaebehoppen* means Flaebe's
horse). Lunn bred her to Frederiksborgs
and she founded a line of spotted horses,
largely through her grandson Mikkel.
• **CHARACTERISTICS** The old
Knabstrupers were tough, rawboned
horses. They were intelligent, tractable,
and quick to learn. They deteriorated
as a result of injudicious breeding for
color, and now hardly exist. The
modern type, closer in character to
the Appaloosa, is a quality animal
of some substance and with a
greater range of colors.

DENMARK

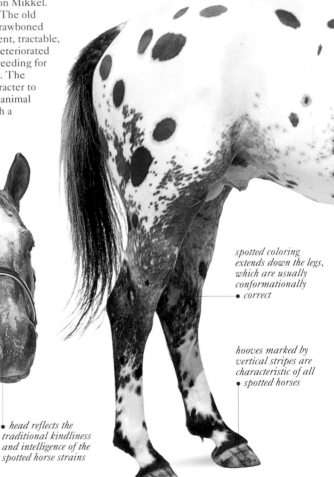

*spotted coloring
extends down the legs,
which are usually
conformationally
• correct*

*hooves marked by
vertical stripes are
characteristic of all
• spotted horses*

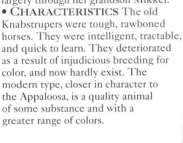

*• head reflects the
traditional kindliness
and intelligence of the
spotted horse strains*

Colors Spotted	Uses Saddle

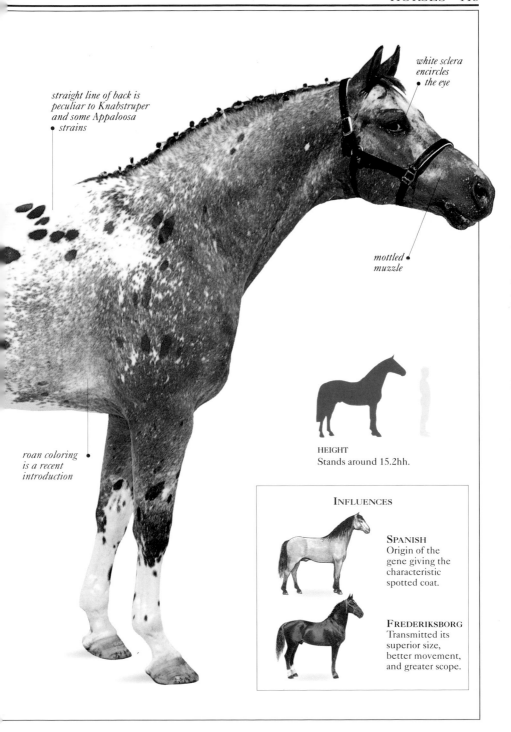

white sclera
encircles
the eye

straight line of back is
peculiar to Knabstruper
and some Appaloosa
strains

mottled
muzzle

roan coloring
is a recent
introduction

HEIGHT
Stands around 15.2hh.

INFLUENCES

SPANISH
Origin of the
gene giving the
characteristic
spotted coat.

FREDERIKSBORG
Transmitted its
superior size,
better movement,
and greater scope.

Environment Temperate, Controlled	Origin 20th century		Blood Warm

DANISH WARMBLOOD

One of the more recent of the selectively bred European competition horses is the Danish Warmblood, whose studbook was not opened until the 1960s. In a relatively short space of time, however, Danish breeders have succeeded in producing a competition horse of superior quality and more versatility than many of the European breeds.

DENMARK

• **BREEDING** Denmark has an ancient equestrian tradition. Cistercian monks in 14th-century Holstein (a Danish Duchy until 1864) crossed the best Spanish stock with north German mares. One of the results was Denmark's Frederiksborg. The Danish Warmblood was founded on Frederiksborg stock, crossed with the Thoroughbred. The resultant local mares were bred to Anglo-Norman (virtually Selle Français) stallions, Thoroughbreds, and Trakehners. The mix was adjusted to produce a sound horse of excellent conformation, relatively fixed in type, and with scope and galloping ability. The Hanoverian influence is absent in the Danish Warmblood, which may account for its distinctive character compared to other warmbloods.

• **CHARACTERISTICS** The best Danish horses have a Thoroughbred outline that is combined with substance, strength, and good legs. They are courageous and spirited, have excellent temperaments, and good, free action. They are brilliant dressage horses and first-class performers in cross country.

INFLUENCES

FREDERIKSBORG
The base stock, a showy carriage and riding horse of some elegance.

TRAKEHNER
Used for its fixed type, correct conformation, and proven ability.

THOROUGHBRED
An upgrading influence; gave quality, speed, and improved action.

shape of hoof and corresponding slope of pastern are exactly • correct

Colors All solid		Uses Saddle

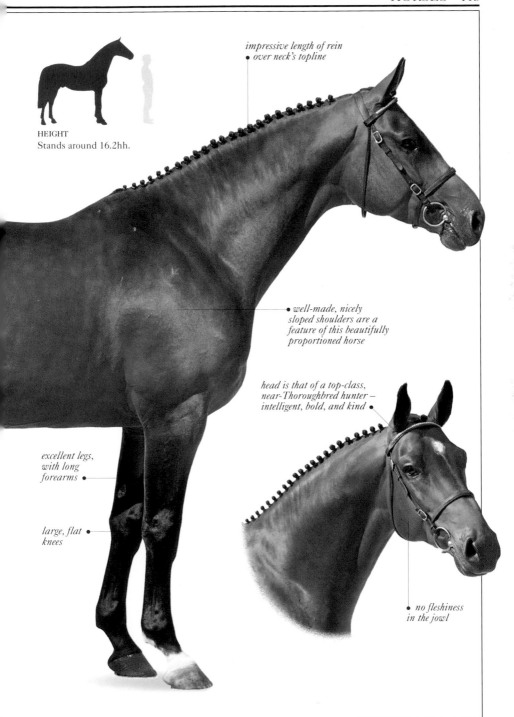

HEIGHT
Stands around 16.2hh.

*impressive length of rein
over neck's topline*

*well-made, nicely
sloped shoulders are a
feature of this beautifully
proportioned horse*

*head is that of a top-class,
near-Thoroughbred hunter –
intelligent, bold, and kind*

*excellent legs,
with long
forearms*

*large, flat
knees*

*no fleshiness
in the jowl*

Environment Cool temperate	Origin Pre-Christian	Blood Cold

FRIESIAN

The black Friesian is a coldblood horse of ancient origin. In its own land it arouses much the same admiration, and even adulation, as that given to the massive Shire horse in Britain. Although it is ridden and displays great agility under saddle, the modern Friesian excels as an impressive, free-moving harness horse. Its temperament and appearance made it popular with circus trainers, and its presence and color ensure a market for it in the funeral business.

NETHERLANDS: FRIESLAND

• **BREEDING** The Friesian, which descends from the "primitive" Forest Horse of Europe, is bred principally in Friesland on the northern Netherlands coast. It carried the German and Friesian Knights to the Crusades, and was used as an all-purpose warhorse. At first it was improved by crossings with oriental horses, and thereafter, up to the Netherlands becoming independent of Spain in 1609, it was much influenced by the pervading Spanish blood. As the flank guard of the Roman legions, Friesian horses played a role in the development of the British Dales and Fell ponies. Thereafter, through the Old English Black, they influenced the Shire. Both the Oldenburg and the Døle Gudbrandsdal have strong Friesian connections.

• **CHARACTERISTICS** The Friesian is noted for its lovable character and easy temperament. Constitutionally, it is robust and it can be kept very economically.

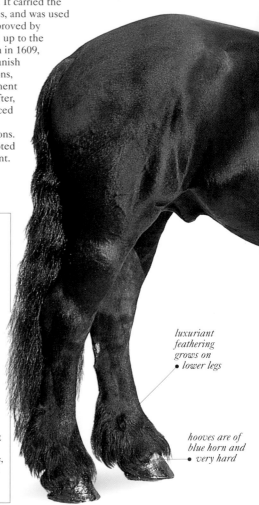

luxuriant feathering grows on • lower legs

hooves are of blue horn and • very hard

INFLUENCES

SPANISH
Much improved the carriage and added quality and refinement.

BARB
Transmitted its great stamina, fiery character, and endurance.

FOREST HORSE
Passed on the typical, primitive, heavy base stock characteristics.

Colors Black	Uses Harness

HEIGHT
Stands at 15hh or more.

*neck is arched and
carried proudly*

*strong shoulders
are characteristic*

*thick, full
mane*

*head is long, ears are
short, and expression
is alert and kindly*

Environment Cool temperate	Origin 19th century	Blood Warm

GELDERLANDER

Of the two principal components in the makeup of the
Dutch Warmblood, the Groningen and the Gelderlander,
the latter is the more attractive. The marketwise breeders
of Holland's Gelder province created it to fulfill their own
needs, and at the same time to be attractive to their
neighbors and remain a distinctive type.

• **BREEDING** About a century ago, the Gelder breeders
saw a market for a showy carriage horse of presence that
would do light work on the farm and could also be used as
a sensible saddle horse. To obtain this, while retaining the
essential docility of character, they introduced a variety
of bloods to their common native mares. They used the
Norfolk Roadster, as well as German, Polish, Hanoverian,
and Russian crosses (the latter predominantly eastern).
When they had fixed the type, they added Cleveland Bay,
Oldenburg, and Anglo-Norman blood. Then, to improve
quality, they introduced Thoroughbred and Arabian.

• **CHARACTERISTICS** The modern Gelderlander
is both an upstanding, powerful carriage horse of the
best type and a useful heavyweight riding horse
with some jumping ability.

NETHERLANDS: GELDER
PROVINCE

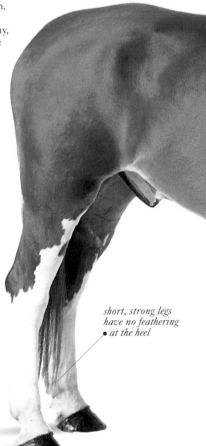

*short, strong legs
have no feathering
• at the heel*

*head is not •
beautiful, but
has an honest
outlook, with a
calm, intelligent
expression*

Colors Chestnut	Uses Saddle, Light Draft, Carriage

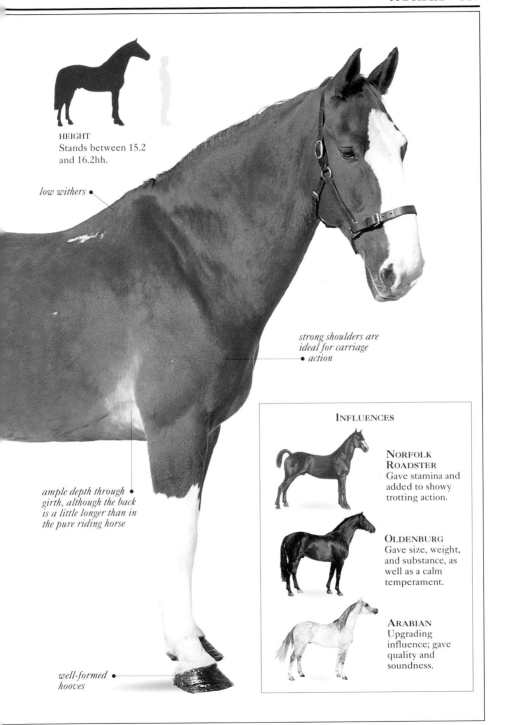

HEIGHT
Stands between 15.2
and 16.2hh.

low withers

*strong shoulders are
ideal for carriage
action*

*ample depth through
girth, although the back
is a little longer than in
the pure riding horse*

*well-formed
hooves*

INFLUENCES

**NORFOLK
ROADSTER**
Gave stamina and
added to showy
trotting action.

OLDENBURG
Gave size, weight,
and substance, as
well as a calm
temperament.

ARABIAN
Upgrading
influence; gave
quality and
soundness.

Environment Cool temperate	Origin 19th century	Blood Warm

GRONINGEN

The Groningen has the distinction of providing, along with the Gelderlander, the base stock for the evolution of the very successful Dutch Warmblood. Today, it can hardly be said to still exist in its old form but, in its time, the Groningen was an essentially practical animal bred to meet the specific agricultural needs of the region.

• **BREEDING** The breed originated in the Groningen region of the Netherlands. Up to 1945 the Groningen was a heavy farmhorse type that could double as a steady but not spectacular coach horse. It was noted for the strength of its quarters, but was not distinguished by the freedom of its action. Thereafter, it was improved and lightened as the demand for a more active, versatile horse increased.

• **CHARACTERISTICS** The old Groningen breed relied heavily on its famous neighbor, the Friesian, and the powerful, temperate Oldenburg. From these two it inherited its calm character and willing disposition. The roomy Groningen mares, when crossed with quality sires, produced strong stock, passing on both their size and good bone.

NETHERLANDS:
GRONINGEN REGION

like many coach-type horses, it is fairly long in body and back

plain, honest head is carried on a short, strong neck, which characterizes the heavier carriage horse

Colors Bay, Brown	Uses Light Draft, Coach

HEIGHT
Stands between 15.2 and 16.2hh.

*originally not a good fronted
horse, it was much improved
• in this respect after 1945*

*joints were once
inclined to be round
and fleshy, but there
was ample bone •*

INFLUENCES

FRIESIAN
Gave endurance
and better legs to
the common
Dutch mares.

OLDENBURG
Passed on size,
strength, bone,
and power in
the quarters.

Environment Cool temperate	Origin 20th century	Blood Warm

DUTCH WARMBLOOD

The Dutch Warmblood is one of the most successful of the post war competition horses, and one of the most skillfully promoted. Marius, sire of the fabulous Milton, was an exceptional representative of the breed and has to be regarded as one of the great show-jumping stallions of recent years. Dutch Courage, the dressage horse produced by the British Olympic rider Jennie Loriston-Clarke, was significant in establishing the breed's reputation in Britain.

NETHERLANDS

• BREEDING Essentially, the Dutch Warmblood is the product of an amalgamation of two of Holland's indigenous breeds, the Gelderlander and the Groningen. The former is a good-moving carriage horse of presence that can also be used under saddle; the latter is heavier and has very powerful quarters. When they were combined, the base for a competition horse was created. This base was refined with Thoroughbred blood, and the mix was subsequently adjusted, in respect of temperament and conformation, by crosses with French and German warmbloods.

• CHARACTERISTICS A proven performer as a show jumper and dressage horse, the Dutch Warmblood is noted for its strong legs and hooves. Although not fast, the breed is athletic with pronounced gymnastic ability. Breeders put much emphasis on the correctness of the action and the even temperament.

• *good, sound legs are a feature of the breed, along with adequate bone*

INFLUENCES

GELDERLANDER
Gave size, strength of shoulder, presence, and a showy action.

GRONINGEN
Increased substance, adding to the power of the quarters.

THOROUGHBRED
Shortened carriage back, improved conformation, and added courage.

Colors All solid	Uses Saddle

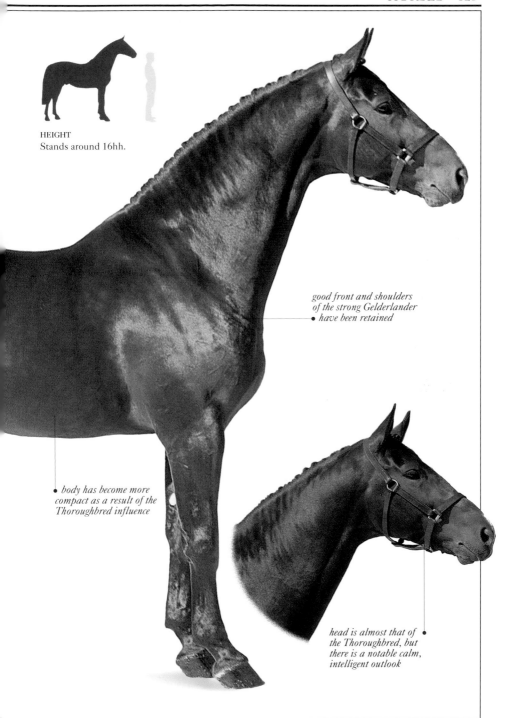

HEIGHT
Stands around 16hh.

good front and shoulders
of the strong Gelderlander
• have been retained

• body has become more
compact as a result of the
Thoroughbred influence

head is almost that of •
the Thoroughbred, but
there is a notable calm,
intelligent outlook

Environment Cool temperate	Origin 20th century	Blood Warm

BELGIAN WARMBLOOD

The Belgian Warmblood is a relatively recent development.
Purpose bred for competition, it excels as a dressage or
jumping horse. Traditionally, Belgium specialized in the
production of heavy agricultural horses, but now upward
of 4,500 Belgian Warmblood foals are born each year.

• **BREEDING** The history of the breed began in the 1950s,
when lighter agricultural horses were crossed with imported
Gelderlanders to produce riding horses. Ten years later, the
Gelderlanders were replaced by the more wiry and athletic
Selle Français and some Hanoverian sires. The importance
of Thoroughbred and Anglo-Arab blood was recognized as a
means of giving quality, and some use is also made of Dutch
Warmblood stallions, horses with impressive performance
records, noted for their equable disposition.

• **CHARACTERISTICS** The amalgam of the various
bloods has resulted in powerful, straight-moving horses
of great agility and excellent temperaments. Belgian
Warmblood breeders enjoy a considerable demand for
these reliable horses and they have developed
flourishing export markets.

BELGIUM

INFLUENCES

GELDERLANDER
Provided size,
strength, and
substance, as
well as bone.

**SELLE
FRANÇAIS**
Gave athletic
ability, stamina,
and hardiness.

HANOVERIAN
Gave correctness
of movement,
size, and equable
temperament.

THOROUGHBRED
Improved speed,
conformation, and
freedom of action;
gave high courage.

Colors All solid	Uses Saddle

HEIGHT
Stands around 16.2hh.

withers are particularly well-placed

despite the Gelderlander background, shoulders are free from any coaching character

good depth to the compact, well-sprung barrel and no hint of too much length in the back

breeders pay much attention to correctness of legs and sound- ness of hooves

head is alert and full of quality, showing the Thoroughbred and Anglo-Arab influence

Environment Cool temperate	Origin 13th century	Blood Warm

TRAKEHNER

Many consider the Trakehner to be Europe's finest warmblood and the ideal competition horse. During World War II, 1,200 Trakehners, out of 25,000 registered in the East Prussian studbook, were trekked 900 miles (1,450 km) across Europe to prevent them from falling into Soviet hands. Using this nucleus, German breeders have been able to preserve the breed.

POLAND: EAST

• **BREEDING** The Trakehner originated in the 13th-century studs of the Teutonic Knights, in what used to be East Prussia. They used indigenous Schweiken ponies, descendants of the Tarpan, as a base. The Royal Trakehner Stud was founded by Friedrich Wilhelm I of Prussia in 1732, and aimed to produce active coach horses. Within 50 years, more emphasis was placed on breeding cavalry remounts. As a result, Thoroughbreds and Arabians were used. The greatest Thoroughbred influence was that of Perfectionist, son of the 1896 Derby and St. Leger winner, Persimmon. Perfectionist's son, Tempelhuter, provided a powerful line for the Trakehner. Tempelhuter daughters are the base of Dingo, the other important Trakehner line.

• **CHARACTERISTICS** Selective breeding has ensured excellent conformation. The Trakehner has the appearance of a top-class middleweight hunter, and is courageous across country. It excels at dressage and show jumping.

• *good, strong legs and joints*

INFLUENCES

ARABIAN
The upgrading influence that ensured a good temperament.

THOROUGHBRED
Improved the size, also giving the Trakehner greater speed and scope.

SCHWEIKEN
The indigenous base stock, passing on primitive vigor.

Colors All solid	Uses Saddle

HEIGHT
Stands between
16 and 17.2hh.

*strong, sloped
shoulders and long,
elegant neck are
• particularly notable*

*• outline of strong body
inclines toward the
Thoroughbred and
indicates speed and
athletic ability*

*hooves are harder and
pasterns more correctly
sloped than in many
other warmbloods •*

*head reflects strong •
Thoroughbred element
and is full of quality
and very expressive*

Environment Cool temperate	Origin 20th century	Blood Warm

WIELKOPOLSKI

The Wielkopolski embraces the two older, dual-purpose, warmblood horses of central and western Poland – the Poznan and the Masuren, neither of which now exists officially. It is typical of Poland's long horse tradition, being practical, economical, and depending to a degree on the Arabian blood that is so much a part of the Polish heritage.

• **BREEDING** The Poznan Horse, established in the state studs about 150 years ago, was an amalgam of Arabian, Thoroughbred, and Hanoverian blood, with a later cross to the Trakehner. The Masuren, bred in the Masury district was, to all intents, Trakehner in origin. The two distinctive strains were combined in the Wielkopolski, and crosses were made to the Thoroughbred, Arabian, and Anglo-Arab.

• **CHARACTERISTICS** The Wielkopolski is a strong, quality horse that can be used in harness or under saddle. Heavier specimens, combining activity and the characteristic good temperament, can be used as farm horses. The handsome Wielkopolski is noted for its paces: long, easy walk; low, level trot; and ground-covering canter and gallop.

POLAND: CENTRAL AND WESTERN

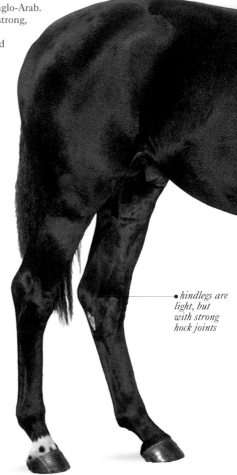

• *hindlegs are light, but with strong hock joints*

INFLUENCES

TRAKEHNER
Added quality, improved action, and reinforced the constitution.

HANOVERIAN
Gave size, substance, and bone; added to equable temperament.

ARABIAN
Gave refinement, spirit, and soundness of leg and constitution.

THOROUGHBRED
Improved speed, action, and competitive ability.

Colors All solid	Uses Saddle, Harness, Light Draft

HEIGHT
Stands between 16
and 16.2hh.

shoulders in this muscular
horse are well-sloped
• and very strong

body is deep, •
compact, and
powerfully built

head is handsome, showing •
combined influence of the
Arabian, Anglo-Arab, and
Thoroughbred crosses

Environment Cool temperate	Origin 10th–11th centuries	Blood Warm

BAVARIAN WARMBLOOD

The Bavarian is not the best known of the German warmbloods but it is one of the oldest, and its origins trace back to the Crusades. At the time of the Crusades, it was known as the Rottaler, the chestnut warhorse of the Rott Valley in Germany, a noted breeding area.

• **BREEDING** The horses were bred at the monastery studs during the 16th century, and 200 years later stock was being upgraded by imported halfbreed English stallions, Cleveland Bays, and some Normans. A century after, the Oldenburg was used to increase the substance of the breed, laying the foundation for the modern, more scopey, competition horse.

• **CHARACTERISTICS** The Bavarian is of medium size with great depth and width, in proportion. Breeders place great emphasis on temperament, and the stock is tested carefully for performance.

INFLUENCES

CLEVELAND Provided size, strength, substance, and stamina.

OLDENBURG Gave substance and improved correctness of leg.

THOROUGHBRED Gave additional speed, quality, and courage; improved scope.

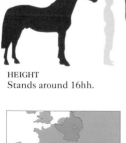

HEIGHT
Stands around 16hh.

GERMANY: ROTT VALLEY, BAVARIA

• *strongly built body combines bone, substance, and depth through girth*

Colors Chestnut	Uses Saddle

Environment Cool temperate	Origin 18th century	Blood Warm

HANOVERIAN

Foremost among the German competition horses is the Hanoverian, a great show-jumping breed and a dressage performer of note.

- **BREEDING** Selective breeding began in 1735, when George II, Elector of Hanover and King of England, founded the Celle stud. Initially, 14 Holsteiner stallions were used with local mares to produce all-around farm horses. Then Thoroughbreds were used to produce a better quality horse. After World War II, emphasis changed towards competition, and both Trakehner and Thoroughbred blood was employed to obtain further refinement, but crossing was carefully controlled.
- **CHARACTERISTICS** The policy of strict selection produces a horse of exceptional strength with notably correct movement, and a particularly good temperament.

INFLUENCES

THOROUGHBRED
Gave courage, and improved speed, conformation, and movement.

HOLSTEIN
Fulfilled the original need for size, strength, and substance.

TRAKEHNER
Passed on strength of constitution and stamina.

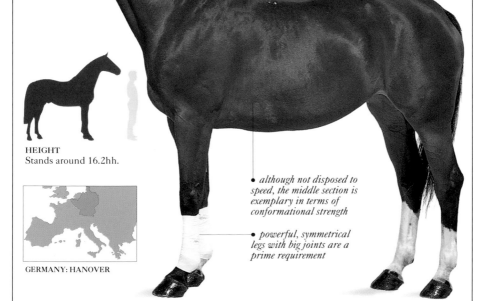

HEIGHT
Stands around 16.2hh.

GERMANY: HANOVER

• *although not disposed to speed, the middle section is exemplary in terms of conformational strength*

• *powerful, symmetrical legs with big joints are a prime requirement*

Colors All solid	Uses Saddle

Environment Cool temperate	Origin 17th–19th century	Blood Warm

HOLSTEINER

The Holsteiner has been refined by the increasing use of the Thoroughbred cross, and is probably the best cross country prospect of the carefully bred German warmbloods. The Holsteiner is also an impressive dressage horse, and some of the best post-war German show jumpers have been Holsteiners.

• **BREEDING** During the 17th century, the Holsteiner was in demand as a heavy, but not inelegant, coach horse. The horses of that time were an amalgam of German and Spanish blood, topped with an oriental infusion. In the 19th century, the Yorkshire Coach Horse was introduced. After this, as more emphasis was placed on producing a riding horse, more reliance was put on Thoroughbred crosses.

• **CHARACTERISTICS** The modern Holsteiner exhibits very correct, straight, and rhythmic paces. Some knee action, however, is acceptable. The heaviness that typified the old Holsteiner has disappeared. The tractable, intelligent, and reliable Holsteiner is also a bold jumper.

GERMANY: HOLSTEINER

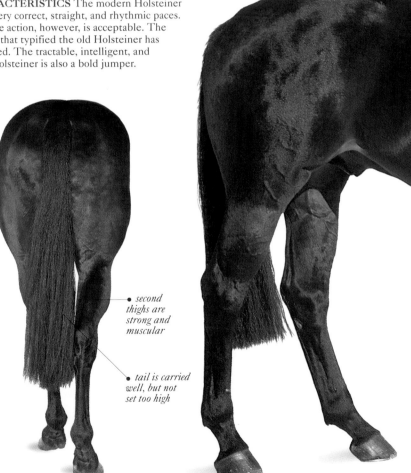

• *second thighs are strong and muscular*

• *tail is carried well, but not set too high*

Colors All solid	Uses Saddle

*shoulder blades are
not widely spaced*

*withers are
relatively high*

*throat should be
clean, with no
fleshiness in the jowl*

*neck is long and
slightly arched*

*correct legs and a good
hoof structure are
always sought by
Holsteiner breeders*

HEIGHT
Stands between 16 and 17hh.

INFLUENCES

THOROUGHBRED
Courage, speed,
and improved
action were all
introduced.

YORKSHIRE
COACH HORSE
Gave substance,
bone, size, and
greater strength.

Environment Temperate, Controlled	Origin 17th century		Blood Warm

OLDENBURG

The Oldenburg was developed in the 17th century as a coach
horse, able to cope with rough roadways, and capable of doing
a variety of agricultural jobs. Since then the breed has been
continually adapted by skillful and controlled breeding to
meet changing requirements. Still the most powerfully built
of the warmbloods, the Oldenburg is a competition horse,
particularly suited for dressage and driving.

GERMANY: OLDENBURG

• **BREEDING** The breed, based on Friesian stock,
originated in the provinces of Oldenburg and East Friesland, now in Germany. It was developed by Count Anton
Gunther von Oldenburg (1603–1667), who used Spanish
and Neapolitan blood. Halfbreed English stallions were
introduced at the end of the 18th century, and then
Thoroughbreds and some Cleveland Bays around
1897. An important outcross was Normann 700, a
Norman from Norfolk Roadster and English
halfbreed lines. When emphasis shifted to the
riding horse, another Norman, Condor, was
used, as well as the Thoroughbred, Lupus.
Recent crosses have also been Thoroughbred,
with occasional recourse to the Hanoverian.

• **CHARACTERISTICS** The modern
Oldenburg is an impressive horse, with an
equable temper. It retains some knee
action, but has correct, rhythmic paces.
Surprisingly for such a large-framed horse,
the breed matures early.

*hooves are
uniformly well-
shaped and in
proportion* •

INFLUENCES

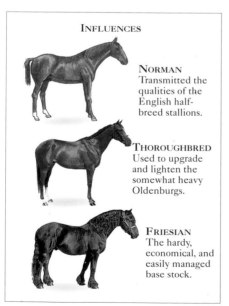

NORMAN
Transmitted the
qualities of the
English half-
breed stallions.

THOROUGHBRED
Used to upgrade
and lighten the
somewhat heavy
Oldenburgs.

FRIESIAN
The hardy,
economical, and
easily managed
base stock.

Colors All solid	Uses Saddle, Harness

HEIGHT
Stands between 16.2 and
17.2hh.

some
thickness in
the jowl

strong neck and long
shoulders still incline
towards coach horse
conformation

chest is both
broad and wide

exceptionally
powerful body

head has a kind, genuine
appearance and profile is
straight or inclined to a
Roman nose

Environment Cool temperate	Origin 16th century	Blood Warm

WÜRTTEMBURG

The Württemburg is one of Germany's classic warmblood breeds and has been bred systematically for over a century at the oldest of the German state-owned stud farms at Marbach. This stud was founded in 1573 by Duke Christoph von Württemburg, and in the early 19th century had a horse complement exceeding 81,000.

• **BREEDING** The first influence of note was the Arabian crossed with local warmblood mares of mixed origin. In the 17th century, Barb and Spanish mares were brought in, as well as some of the heavier Friesian stallions. Anglo-Norman and East Prussian blood were helpful in fixing a stocky, all-around type. An Anglo-Norman of the Cob type, called Faust, created the prototype Württemburg. The greatest improvement to the breed was made by Trakehners, and notable among these was Julmond, who died at Marbach in 1965. An interesting feature of the Württemburg, which is not found in the other German warmbloods, is the powerful influence of the famous Marbach herd of Arabians. Although it was originally bred as a light utility horse, more emphasis is now placed on it being suitable for ridden competition.

• **CHARACTERISTICS** The Württemburg is a stocky riding horse with great depth through the girth. It is noted for its sound legs, excellent action, and faultless disposition. A very hardy horse, it is long-lived and exceptionally economical to feed.

GERMANY: MARBACH, WURTTEMBURG

INFLUENCES

ANGLO-NORMAN Gave substance and helped to create the type.

ARABIAN The refining influence, produced the basic type.

TRAKEHNER Gave distinctive size, character, scope, and movement.

Colors Brown, Bay, Chestnut	Uses Saddle

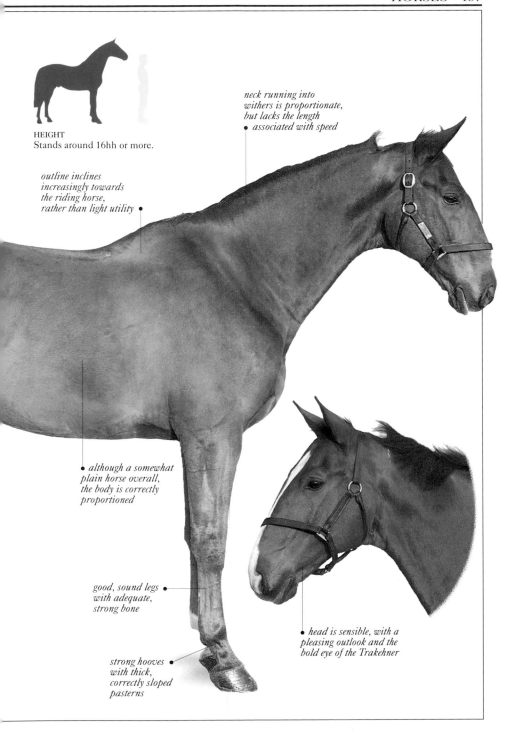

HEIGHT
Stands around 16hh or more.

neck running into withers is proportionate, but lacks the length
• *associated with speed*

outline inclines increasingly towards the riding horse, rather than light utility •

• *although a somewhat plain horse overall, the body is correctly proportioned*

good, sound legs with adequate, strong bone •

strong hooves with thick, correctly sloped pasterns •

• *head is sensible, with a pleasing outlook and the bold eye of the Trakehner*

Environment Cool temperate	Origin 1960s–1970s	Blood Warm

RHINELANDER

The old Rhenish-German or Rhineland heavy draft horse owed much to Brabant blood and was once a popular workhorse throughout the Rhineland, Westphalia, and Saxony. But modern agricultural practice has long since made this breed redundant and it is no longer recognized. However, the Rhenish studbook has moved towards a warmblood riding horse based on the old heavy draft, particularly the lighter specimens.

GERMANY: RHINELAND
AND WESTPHALIA

• **BREEDING** In the 1970s, breeding programs specifically designed to produce a recognizable saddle- or riding-horse type took place. These horses were sired by stallions within the Hanover-Westphalia area, from warmbloods that had Thoroughbred, Trakehner, and Hanoverian blood and that derived, if tenuously, from the old Rhenish background. The modern Rhinelander developed from selected halfbreed stallions which were produced from this amalgam.

• **CHARACTERISTICS** The breeders have concentrated on action and conformation, possibly the hallmark of the German warmbloods, along with the insistence on an equable temperament. Early specimens, however, were said to be lacking in bone, a failure that breeders continually strive to eradicate. The modern Rhinelander is a useful riding horse, although perhaps not, as yet, in the same class as the older established breeds such as the Hanoverian and the Holsteiner.

INFLUENCES

RHINELAND DRAFT
As the base stock, it was responsible for size.

HANOVERIAN
Gave correct movement, good temperament, and riding character.

THOROUGHBRED
Increased scope and speed; acted as an upgrading influence.

Colors All solid, esp. Chestnut	Uses Saddle

HEIGHT
Stands around 16.2hh.

neck is light and
fairly short •

• in this specimen,
the neck runs into a
"bosomy" chest

outline is that of a •
typical riding horse
and, if undistinguished,
is not unattractive

head is sensible, not without •
quality, and reflects equable
temperament

Environment Cool temperate	Origin 19th century	Blood Warm

NONIUS

The Nonius evolved in the 19th century,
when the studs of the vast Austro-Hungarian
Empire, then at its zenith, provided cavalry
remounts throughout Europe.
• **BREEDING** The breed was founded on
Nonius Senior. He was foaled at Calvados,
Normandy, in 1810 and captured by the Hung-
arians in 1813. He was by Orion, an English
halfbreed with Norfolk Roadster blood, out of
a common Norman mare. The type was
obtained by mating the progeny of Arabian,
Lipizzaner, Norman, and English mares by
Nonius back to their sire. In the 1860s, more
Thoroughbred blood was introduced. Today,
Nonius horses are bred in Hortobagy in
Hungary and Topolçianky in Czechoslovakia.
• **CHARACTERISTICS** The Nonius is well-
built and sound. Neither carriage nor saddle
types are fast, but are good all-arounders.

INFLUENCES

ARABIAN
Transmitted its
refinement
and equable
temperament.

NORMAN
Resulted in
increased size
and substance
in the Nonius.

**ENGLISH
HALFBREED**
Gave improved
constitution and
performance.

HEIGHT
Stands between 15.3 and 16.2hh.

*bone below knee is
adequate and legs
are strongly
• proportioned*

*• hard
hooves*

HUNGARY: HORTOBAGY

Colors Bay, Brown	Uses Saddle, Harness

Environment Cool temperate	Origin 19th century	Blood Warm

FURIOSO

The Furioso is closely related to the Nonius and is bred throughout Europe, from Austria to Poland. The Furioso was also bred as a cavalry horse, but it is more refined than the Nonius.

• **BREEDING** The Furioso was founded on two English horses, Furioso and North Star, who were bred to Nonius mares. Furioso, imported in about 1840, was a Thoroughbred. North Star, imported three years later, was the son of the 1834 St. Leger winner, Touchstone, but also had strong Norfolk Roadster connections. He sired many good harness racers. Later, more Thoroughbreds were used. The two lines were crossbred after 1885, when the Furioso strain became more prominent.

• **CHARACTERISTICS** The Furioso is a riding horse of sufficient ability to compete in the major disciplines, including steeplechasing, at European level. It also goes well in harness.

INFLUENCES

NONIUS Provided the base stock for the development of the breed.

THOROUGHBRED An upgrading influence; added size, speed, and improved action.

NORFOLK ROADSTER Ensured stamina, strength, and soundness.

HEIGHT
Stands around 16hh.

HUNGARY: APAJPUSZTA

• *body is compact, and strongly built, with depth through the girth*

hindlegs are strong, • with hocks close to the ground, but they are not built for speed

Colors Black, Brown	Uses Saddle, Harness

Environment Desert	Origin 19th century	Blood Hot

SHAGYA ARAB

The most famous product of the great Hungarian studs of the 19th century is the Shagya Arab, which was bred specifically as a riding horse of quality and substance for the incomparable light cavalry of Hungary. The modern Shagya Arab is just as practical as its forebears, and performs equally as well in harness as it does under saddle. Some of the strains are suitable for use in competitions, including jumping.

HUNGARY: BABOLNA

• **BREEDING** The center of Shagya breeding is the Babolna Stud, founded in 1789. After 1816, Babolna concentrated on the breeding of pure "desert" Arabians and then, increasingly, on halfbreeds of "Arabian Race." These were by pure-bred stallions out of predominantly Arabian mares carrying strains of Spanish, Hungarian, and Thoroughbred blood, and took the name of the breed's foundation stallion, Shagya. This cream-colored horse of Kehil/Siglavi strain was larger than is usual for an Arabian, being 15.2½hh. He arrived at Babolna from Syria in 1836, and his descendants are still at Babolna and other studs in Europe.
• **CHARACTERISTICS** The Shagya is wholly Arabian in outline and character, but it is bigger and has more substance and bone than many of the modern Arabians. The withers are more pronounced and the strong shoulders are more oblique. The hindlegs, often a matter for criticism in the Arabian, are notably correct in the Shagya.

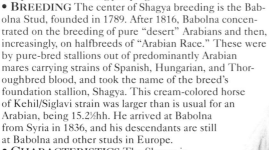

• *remarkably wide forehead*

hindlegs are notably correct •

• *beautiful head, dominated by large eyes*

Colors All solid	Uses Saddle, Harness

outline is that of a high-class Arabian, but frame is larger and more substantial •

• more conventional riding shoulders than those of the Arabian

• compact back, loins, and body are virtually perfect

forelegs are set • well clear of body, ensuring complete freedom of action

HEIGHT
Stands around 15hh.

INFLUENCE

ARABIAN
Arabian prepotency played a large part in Shagya development.

Environment Cool temperate	Origin 16th century	Blood Warm

LIPIZZANER

The Lipizzaner is associated with Vienna's Spanish Riding
School, the School horses are raised at Piber, near Graz in
Austria. It is also bred extensively in Hungary, Romania,
Czechoslovakia, and Slovenia, each country producing its
own type, and in lesser numbers elsewhere in Europe.

• **BREEDING** The Lipizzaner descends from Spanish
horses, taking its name from the stud at Lipica, in Slovenia.
The stud was founded in 1580, when the Hapsburg
Archduke, Charles II, imported 9 stallions and 24 mares from
the Iberian Peninsula. He wanted to ensure a supply
of showy, predominantly white horses for the ducal stables at
Graz and the court stables in Vienna. The Spanish School, so
called because it used only "Spanish" horses, was founded
for the instruction of the nobility in 1572. The present
School, the Winter Riding Hall, was completed in 1735.

• **CHARACTERISTICS** The conformation of the
Lipizzaner is that of a useful, all-around cob. Today,
many Lipizzaners are used as much in harness as
under saddle. The Hungarian-bred horses are superb
carriage horses and, due to Thoroughbred influence,
have more scope and freedom of movement. The
breed is long-lived, many School horses continuing
to perform difficult movements in their twenties.

SLOVENIA: LIPICA

head shows •
Arabian influence, but
retains something of the
hawklike profile of the old
Spanish Horse

Colors Gray	Uses Saddle, Harness

*neck is thick
and quite short*

*withers are not
pronounced, and
action tends to be high*

*shoulders, matching
the formation of the neck,
are as well-suited to
harness as to saddle*

*legs of the long-lived
Lipizzaner are short
and powerful with
good bone*

HEIGHT
Stands between 15.1 and 16.2hh.

*hard
hooves*

INFLUENCE

SPANISH
Contributed its
natural elegance,
strength, and
resilient spirit.

Environment Cool temperate	Origin 19th–20th century	Blood Warm

SELLE FRANCAIS

The French warmblood, called *le cheval de selle Français*, is one of the toughest and most versatile European competition horse breeds.
• **BREEDING** During the 19th century, Norman breeders imported Thoroughbred and halfbreed stallions from England to cross with their useful, but common, Norman stock. This produced the forerunners of the present French Trotter and the Selle Français breeds. After World War II, the Selle Français was further developed using Trotters, Thoroughbreds, Arabians, and Anglo-Arabs.
• **CHARACTERISTICS** The Selle Français was developed as a show jumper and has, perhaps as a result of the Trotter influence, great ability in this field. It is also a highly courageous horse, well able to compete in crosscountry racing and eventing.

INFLUENCES

NORMAN
The base stock which passed on its constitution and added size.

ARABIAN
Added refinement; gave spirit and greater physical soundness.

THOROUGHBRED
Contributed to speed; improved action and overall mental stamina.

HEIGHT
Stands around 16hh.

very strong legs have bone measurement of not less than 8 in (20 cm)

FRANCE: NORMANDY

Colors All solid	Uses Saddle

Environment Cool temperate	Origin 19th century	Blood Warm

FRENCH TROTTER

The sport of trotting was established in France in the 19th century, encouraging the evolution of the French Trotter.

• **BREEDING** The utilitarian Norman horse provided the base for the Trotter strains. The principal outside influences were The Norfolk Phenomenon, a Norfolk Roadster; Young Rattler, a Thoroughbred/Roadster cross; and, to a lesser extent, Heir of Linne, a Thoroughbred. Later, to improve the speed, crosses were made to the American Standardbred.

• **CHARACTERISTICS** This tough breed races in the diagonal gait and is able to take on the best harness racers. In 1989, the qualifying standard for four-year-olds and over was 1 minute 22 seconds over three-fifths of a mile (1 kilometer).

INFLUENCES

NORFOLK ROADSTER Gave stamina, robust constitution, trotting ability.

NORMAN Base stock; gave size, versatility, and equable temperament.

THOROUGHBRED Contributed to speed, improved action, and overall mental stamina.

fairly flat, trotting withers •

modern French Trotter has good harness shoulders •

HEIGHT
Stands around 16.2hh.

immensely powerful quarters •

legs and hooves are exceptionally hard, strong, and enduring •

FRANCE: NORMANDY

Colors All solid	Uses Harness

Environment Salt marshland	Origin Prehistoric	Blood Warm

CAMARGUE

Camargue horses, known as "the white horses of the sea," are indigenous to the Rhône delta in southern France. Here the *manades* (semi-wild herds) live in much the same way as they have done for thousands of years on the wild, watery wasteland dominated by the *mistral* (the salt-laden wind). Camargue horses are the traditional mounts of the *gardian* (Camargue cowboy), and are indispensable for working the wild, black bulls of the Camargue.

• **BREEDING** It is possible that the Camargue horses are descendants of the prehistoric animals whose remains were discovered at Solutré in the 19th century. Certainly, the breed bears a resemblance to the primitive horses depicted in the Lascaux cave drawings, dated around 15,000 BC. The indigenous horse was undoubtedly influenced by Barbs, brought over from North Africa with the Moorish invaders. Since then, the isolation of the region has ensured that the *manades* have been untouched by outside influences.

• **CHARACTERISTICS** Although hardly a model of conformation, the breed is strong and enduring, and is fiery and courageous under saddle. It is also incredibly hardy and able to exist on the feed offered by stunted reed beds. The action is peculiar – walk, canter, and gallop are free and active, while the trot is so stilted that it is rarely used.

FRANCE: CAMARGUE

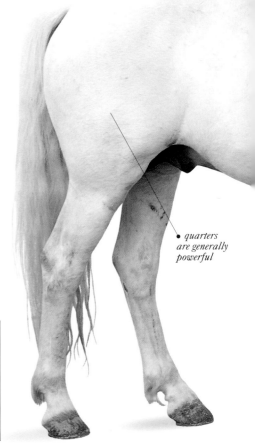

sloped croup and
• *low-set tail*

• *quarters are generally powerful*

HEIGHT
Stands up to 14.2hh.

INFLUENCE

BARB
The powerful genes contributed by the Barb are in evidence.

Colors Gray, White	Uses Saddle

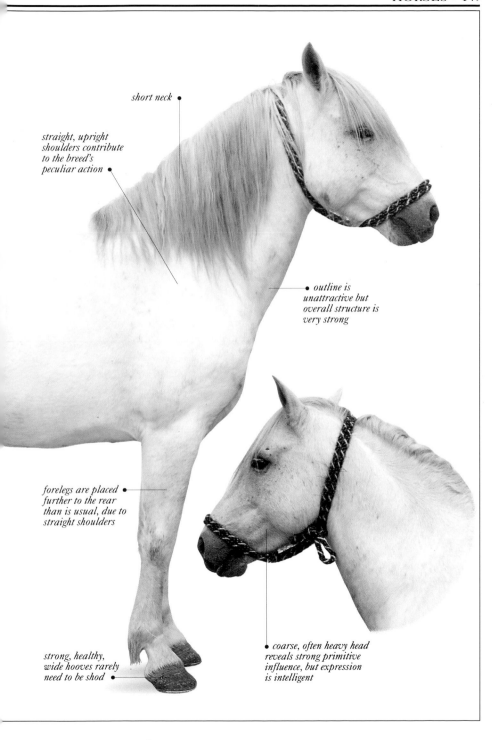

short neck

straight, upright
shoulders contribute
to the breed's
peculiar action

outline is
unattractive but
overall structure is
very strong

forelegs are placed
further to the rear
than is usual, due to
straight shoulders

strong, healthy,
wide hooves rarely
need to be shod

coarse, often heavy head
reveals strong primitive
influence, but expression
is intelligent

Environment Temperate, Controlled	Origin 19th century	Blood Hot

ANGLO-ARAB

The Anglo-Arab is an offshoot of the Arabian and its derivative, the Thoroughbred. It is a horse that should combine the best of both. Such a cross might be expected to inherit some of the Arabian's qualities of soundness and stamina while incorporating the speed and scope of the Thoroughbred, without its sometimes excitable temperament.

• **BREEDING** The breed may be said to have originated in Britain and to have been perfected in France, where Anglo-Arabs have been bred systematically at the great studs of Pau, Pompadour, Tarbes, and Gelos for over 150 years. Britain has produced some good Anglo-Arabs, but their influence on breeding generally is insignificant in comparison with the French product. The British Anglo-Arab is a cross between a Thoroughbred and an Arabian mare or vice versa, with their subsequent recrossings. In 1836, French Anglo-Arab breeding was based on two Arabian stallions – Massoud and Aslan, and three Thoroughbred mares – Dair, Common Mare, and Selim Mare. Entry to the studbook is now confined to horses with a minimum of 25 percent Arabian blood, and ancestors must be Arabian, Thoroughbred, or Anglo-Arab.

• **CHARACTERISTICS** The Anglo-Arab tends more toward the Thoroughbred than the Arabian in appearance. The profile is straight, the shoulders are sloped, and the withers are prominent. Although the Anglo-Arab is not as fast as the Thoroughbred, the proportions are those associated with galloping ability. Overall, the Anglo-Arab is bigger and more substantial than the Arabian. In France, Anglo-Arabs have special races; they also jump, event, and compete in dressage competitions at international standard.

UK, AND FRANCE: SOUTHWEST

length in finely formed legs indicates galloping • ability

INFLUENCES

THOROUGHBRED Imparted size, scope, galloping ability, and competitive potential.

ARABIAN Gave soundness, stamina, and endurance, with a kindly temper.

Colors Bay to Chestnut	Uses Saddle

HEIGHT
Stands between 16 and
16.2hh.

• *no fleshiness at the
jowl, and throat is less
thick than the Arabian's*

• *riding shoulders
are virtually those of
the Thoroughbred*

*legs are
sound and
uniformly
good* •

dense, good •
quality bone

long, lean head, with •
*straight profile, reflects
Thoroughbred influence*

Environment Cool temperate	Origin 17th–18th century	Blood Hot

THOROUGHBRED

The Thoroughbred is the fastest and most valuable of the world's horses and supports a huge, multinational breeding and racing industry. The Thoroughbred is also the essential element in the production of competition horses, and the principal means of improving many other breeds.

• **BREEDING** The breed evolved in England in the 17th and 18th centuries when native "running horses" were crossed with oriental stallions. The foundation horses were the Byerley Turk (1689), the Darley Arabian (1704), and the Godolphin Arabian (1728). They produced the four principal Thoroughbred lines: Herod, Eclipse, Matchem, and Highflyer, who was Herod's son.

• **CHARACTERISTICS** A horse of great quality, the Thoroughbred has near-perfect proportions, which are long in comparison with those of more heavily built breeds. It has great athletic ability, and physical and mental stamina. Thoroughbreds are courageous in the extreme, but they are highly strung and sometimes have difficult temperaments.

UK: ENGLAND

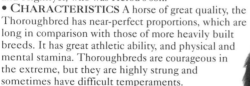

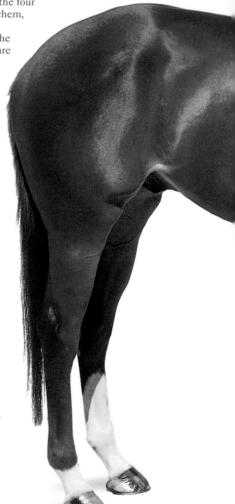

• *quarters are powerful*

• *hindlegs are long for speed*

Colors All solid	Uses Saddle

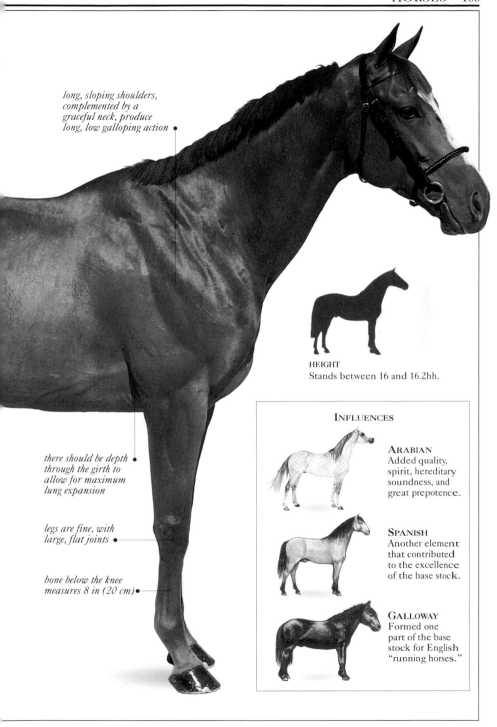

long, sloping shoulders, complemented by a graceful neck, produce long, low galloping action

there should be depth through the girth to allow for maximum lung expansion

legs are fine, with large, flat joints

bone below the knee measures 8 in (20 cm)

HEIGHT
Stands between 16 and 16.2hh.

INFLUENCES

ARABIAN
Added quality, spirit, hereditary soundness, and great prepotence.

SPANISH
Another element that contributed to the excellence of the base stock.

GALLOWAY
Formed one part of the base stock for English "running horses."

Environment Cool temperate	Origin 19th century	Blood Warm

HACKNEY HORSE

The modern Hackney Horse is the most spectacular show ring harness horse, although it also takes part successfully in competitive driving events at international level. It is an English breed, derived from the renowned Norfolk and Yorkshire Roadsters, and has been exported all over Europe as well as to the Americas, South Africa, and Australia. The origin of the word Hackney, used with a capital letter after the foundation of the Hackney Horse Society in 1883, is open to question. It probably comes from the French *haquenée*, which means a "nag" or gelding. Hackney, without the capital letter, was used to describe a riding horse from the Middle Ages onward.

• **BREEDING** Both Yorkshire and Norfolk Roadsters shared a common ancestor in Original Shales, who was by Blaze (foaled in 1733), out of a Norfolk mare. Blaze was a son of the first great racehorse, Flying Childers, and a grandson of the Darley Arabian, one of the foundation sires of the Thoroughbred. The modern Hackney has a strong connection to the Thoroughbred, though its emphasis is on trotting, rather than galloping.

• **CHARACTERISTICS** The Yorkshire and Norfolk Roadsters were used as much under saddle as in harness, and were able to travel long distances at 16–17 mph (26–27 km/h), carrying heavy weights. The main characteristic of the breed is the brilliance of the high, floating action, described by the breed society standard as "effortless, electrical, and snappy at its zenith."

UK: NORFOLK, ENGLAND

tail is set and carried high

hocks have maximum flexion

legs are relatively short, with joints not carried high off the ground

HEIGHT
Stands around 15.3hh.

INFLUENCE

NORFOLK TROTTER
Passed on stamina, trotting ability, and robust constitution.

Colors All solid	Uses Harness

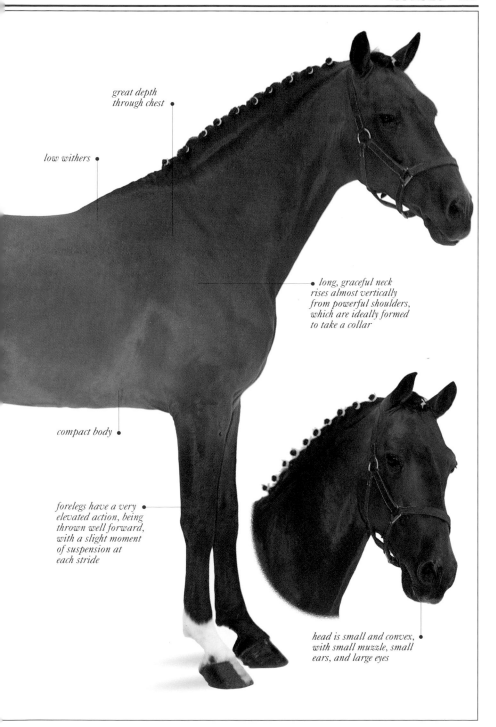

great depth
through chest

low withers

long, graceful neck
rises almost vertically
from powerful shoulders,
which are ideally formed
to take a collar

compact body

forelegs have a very
elevated action, being
thrown well forward,
with a slight moment
of suspension at
each stride

head is small and convex,
with small muzzle, small
ears, and large eyes

Environment Cool temperate	Origin Middle Ages	Blood Warm

CLEVELAND BAY

The Cleveland Bay is the oldest and purest of the indigenous British horse breeds and was used in the 18th and 19th centuries to upgrade many European breeds. In Britain, it has enjoyed royal patronage for over 200 years. The shortage of purebred mares has caused the Rare Breeds Trust to classify the Cleveland Bay situation as "critical."

• **BREEDING** The breed evolved in the Middle Ages from the bay-colored Chapman horses of Cleveland in northern England. Apart from the addition of Spanish and Barb blood in the 17th century, the Cleveland was free from outside influence. The result was a powerful coach horse that could work in heavy mud and carry men hunting in all conditions.

• **CHARACTERISTICS** The breed is long-lived and remarkably prepotent, transmitting size, bone, constitutional hardiness, and usually jumping ability when crossed with the Thoroughbred. It is a magnificent coach horse and is employed as such in the Royal stables.

INFLUENCE

SPANISH Lightened base stock, endowing elegance, spirit, and strength.

HEIGHT
Stands around 16.2hh.

immensely powerful quarters contribute to • jumping ability

• strong neck and shoulders are ideal for carriage work

measurement from • wither to elbow equals or exceeds that from elbow to ground

bone measures • 9 in (22 cm) or more

legs are clean and without • feathering

UK: CLEVELAND, ENGLAND

Colors Bay	Uses Saddle, Harness

Environment Cool temperate	Origin 12th century	Blood Warm

IRISH DRAFT

The Irish Draft, the "horse of the country-side," was used for every type of work on small Irish farms. Although not fast, it was ridden, and it developed an ability to negotiate tricky crosscountry obstacles. Crossed with the Thoroughbred, it produces the world's best crosscountry horse – the Irish hunter. This cross also produces horses that are successful in the show ring and the major ridden disciplines.

• **BREEDING** The size of the indigenous stock was increased by French and Flemish heavy horses in the 12th century, and the type was later upgraded by Spanish horses. The limestone pastures and mild climate of Ireland contribute to the breed's bone and substance.

• **CHARACTERISTICS**
The Irish Draft is a natural, athletic jumper with an equable temper, and is amazingly economical to keep.

INFLUENCES

SPANISH
The upgrading and refining action on the native stock.

FLANDERS
Gave the breed its overall size, weight, and substance.

HEIGHT
Stands between 16 and 17hh.

• *back is long on occasion*

• *riding shoulders have been improved*

• *powerful forehand*

• *overall structure is strong*

• *massive legs*

hooves are usually well-made •

IRELAND

Colors All solid	Uses Saddle, Light Draft

Environment Cool temperate	Origin 11th–12th century	Blood Warm

WELSH COB

The Welsh Cob, with its explosive trotting action, arouses as much fervor in its native land as do the Welsh choirs or rugby football. It is the natural successor to the great trotting tradition of the Norfolk Roadster, which played a part in its evolution. As a harness horse, the Welsh Cob is unsurpassed in stamina and courage and, under saddle, it is a bold ride with great jumping ability.

UK: WALES

• **BREEDING** The Welsh Cob (Section D in the studbook) is, in perfection, a larger version of the Welsh Mountain Pony, which represents its base. These ponies were crossed with Roman imports and then, in the 11th and 12th centuries, with Spanish horses to produce the Powys Cob and a heavier animal, the Welsh Cart Horse. In the 18th and 19th centuries, outcrosses to Norfolk Roadsters and Yorkshire Coach Horses, with a mixture of Arabian blood, resulted in the modern Cob. In the past, there was a big market for the Cobs as gun horses and troopers for mounted infantry. Until the 1960s, Cobs were employed in large numbers on milk, bread, and general delivery rounds in the big cities.

• **CHARACTERISTICS** The Welsh Cob is in demand as a harness and saddle horse, and as a cross with the Thoroughbred to produce competition horses. The Cob is economical to keep, exceptionally hardy, robust in constitution, and inherently sound.

• *powerful quarters*

• *extraordinary flexion in hock joints contributes to brilliant action*

INFLUENCES

WELSH A
The base of Cob breeding; gave movement and soundness.

SPANISH
Improved size and strength, and contributed to horse's carriage.

NORFOLK ROADSTER
Established good trotting ability and gave stamina.

Colors All solid	Uses Harness, Saddle

HEIGHT
Stands between 14.2
and 15.2hh.

*strong, arched neck
joins smoothly with
powerful shoulders*

*head is neat, with
small, pony ears and,
despite the Cob's size, is
full of pony character*

*there is depth through
the girth, and body is
compact, well-sprung in
the ribs, and very strong*

*some silky
feathering at
the heel is
permissible*

Environment Mediterranean	Origin 18th century	Blood Warm

SALERNO

The Salerno, although now much reduced in number, is one of the most attractive of the Italian warmbloods. The homeland of the breed is in the Campania region of Italy, adjoining Puglia. Some notable horses were produced at the Morese Stud, including two of the greatest Italian show jumpers, Merano and Posillipo, both ridden by the Italian Raimondo d'Inzeo.

ITALY: CAMPANIA

• **BREEDING** The Morese Stud is close to where the Bourbon Charles III, King of Naples and then of Spain, founded the stud of Persano in the first half of the 18th century, and it was from this stud that the Salerno evolved. The horses, bred at Persano and called by that name, were based on the Neapolitan. Neapolitans were bred near Sorrento and Naples, and were full of Spanish and Barb blood. They were regarded as the finest school horses of the day and were much admired for their high, fiery action and exceptional strength of leg. These horses were crossed with the local horses of the Salerno and Ofanto valleys, and then use was made of Arabian and Spanish imports to produce a distinctive, quality riding horse. The stud was closed after the establishment of the Italian Republic, and when breeding was revived in 1900, the old name lapsed, the breed being increasingly referred to as the Salerno.

• **CHARACTERISTICS** The introduction of Thoroughbred blood improved the stock and the result was a good type of cavalry horse, bigger than its predecessors, attractive in appearance, with good conformation, and a pronounced aptitude for jumping.

INFLUENCES

SPANISH
Gave strength, agility, improved conformation, and spirit.

THOROUGHBRED
Added size, quality, courage, and greater freedom of action.

Colors All solid	Uses Saddle

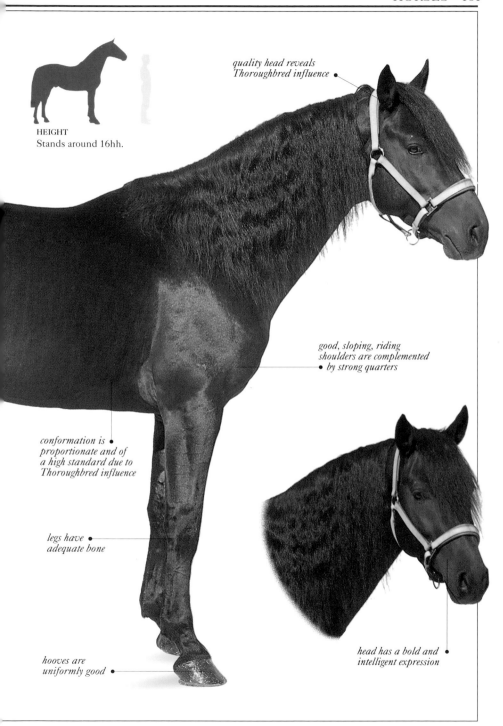

HEIGHT
Stands around 16hh.

*quality head reveals
Thoroughbred influence* •

*good, sloping, riding
shoulders are complemented
• by strong quarters*

conformation is •
*proportionate and of
a high standard due to
Thoroughbred influence*

legs have •
adequate bone

*hooves are
uniformly good* •

head has a bold and •
intelligent expression

Environment Mediterranean	Origin 16th century	Blood Warm

SARDINIAN

Like so many of the Italian breeds, there is little discernible order in the breeding of the Sardinian horse, even though for centuries its home, Sardinia was a principal importer of horses. In 1918, the island's horse population was estimated to be 60,000; some 40 years later the figure had dropped to about 24,000.

• **BREEDING** Without doubt, the breed was founded on crosses between the Barb horses of North Africa and Arabia. Ferdinand the Catholic (1452–1516) introduced Andalusian blood. He established a stud of Spanish horses near Abbasanta and made them available to Sardinian breeders. Studs dedicated to producing a Sardinian horse were founded at Padromannu, Mores, and Monte Minerva, and a distinct type began to appear. However, horse breeding went into a decline when Sardinia passed to the House of Savoy in 1720. In 1908, Arabian stallions were imported to upgrade the stock, with the object of producing the tough, enduring saddle horses for which Sardinia had been famed.

• **CHARACTERISTICS** The Sardinian horse was prized for its hardiness and stamina. In appearance, it is oriental. The best horses have good conformation, whereas others, because of a lack of systematic breeding policies, lack it. It is said that a good Sardinian is bold, intelligent, and jumps well.

ITALY: SARDINIA

quarters are light but the tail is well-positioned •

• *hocks are carried fairly high*

• *hindlegs lack some symmetry*

HEIGHT
Stands around 15.2hh.

INFLUENCE

ARABIAN
The Arabian was the greatest influence in the 20th century.

Colors Bay, Brown	Uses Saddle

neck is in proportion
and, in best specimens,
is gradually curved and
without thickness at jowl •

withers are reasonably
defined, but back tends
to be long and straight •

long, sloped shoulders
retain some oriental
background and are of
• acceptable riding type

build is light but •
tough and wiry,
with sufficient depth
through the girth

longish cannons •

• relatively plain
head is not coarse
or heavy

Environment Mediterranean	Origin 19th century	Blood Warm

MAREMMANA

The Maremmana is the utility horse of Tuscany. As a result of its endurance, good temper, and ability to work cattle, it is the favored mount of the *butteri*, the Italian cowboy. It is also employed in agriculture and was once bred as a troop and police horse.

• **BREEDING** The Maremmana is not a horse of an entirely fixed type, nor is it indigenous to Italy. There has been much crossbreeding against an early background of Neapolitan blood and, during the 19th century, there were infusions of English stock, some of it being of Norfolk Roadster extraction.

• **CHARACTERISTICS** Despite the lack of any planned breeding, the Maremmana has some particular qualities. Although it is not very handsome, it is a solid, steady, and serviceable animal, and it is very versatile and economical to keep.

INFLUENCES

SPANISH
Improved the quality of the base stock and added size.

BARB
Contributed its tenacious spirit, hardiness, and great stamina.

NORFOLK ROADSTER
Improved action and soundness of the Maremmana.

HEIGHT
Stands around 15.3hh.

ITALY: TUSCANY

• *conformation is not generally impressive but the best are well-suited for varied work*

legs have adequate •
bone, and hock and knee joints are well-defined

Colors All solid	Uses Saddle, Light Draft

Environment Mediterranean	Origin 15th–16th century	Blood Warm

MURGESE

The modern Murgese, a light draft horse of
variable type, was fully developed in the 1920s
from an earlier form. Some regard it as the Italian
equivalent of the Irish Draft, though inferior.
• **BREEDING** The breed is from Murge, near
Puglia in Italy, a region once famed for its horses.
There is a background of Neapolitan and
probably also Avelignese and Italian Draft.
• **CHARACTERISTICS** The Murgese is a
useful, easily managed agricultural horse and
a willing worker. It can be used as a base for
better quality riding horses as
it has active movement,
despite its short stride.
The mares are used
to breed strong
mules.

INFLUENCES

NEAPOLITAN
Imparted spirit,
overall physical
soundness, and
useful strength.

AVELIGNESE
Added size and
strength, and
ensured equable
temperament.

*withers are
generally flat
• and lumpy*

*back is strong, without
• undue length*

*quarters tend to •
be insufficiently
developed*

*joints of legs are
sometimes small •*

*strong, hard-
wearing •
hooves*

HEIGHT
Stands between 15 and 16hh.

ITALY: MURGE

Colors Chestnut	Uses Light Draft

Environment Hot temperate	Origin Pre-Ice Age	Blood Warm

ANDALUSIAN

The modern Andalusian is the descendant of the Spanish Horse which, along with the Arabian and the Barb, has exerted the greatest influence on the world horse population. Until the 19th century, the Spanish Horse was the first horse of Europe, and the one on which the classical equitation of the Renaissance schools was based. The Spanish Riding School of Vienna was named after Spanish horses used there, and the famous white Lipizzaners derive directly from horses exported from Spain to Lipica (in Slovenia) during the 16th century. The Spanish Horse was a major influence on almost every breed and is the foundation for most American stock.

SPAIN: JEREZ

• **BREEDING** Andalusian breeding is centered on Jerez de la Frontera, Cordoba, and Seville, where it was preserved by the Carthusian monasteries. The Spanish Horse may have derived from a mix of the indigenous Sorraia stock, with its Tarpan connection, and the Barb horses of the Berber invaders from North Africa.

• **CHARACTERISTICS** The Andalusian is a horse of great presence, and although not fast, it is agile and athletic. It has a noble head, with a characteristic hawklike profile, and the mane and tail are long, luxuriant, and frequently wavy.

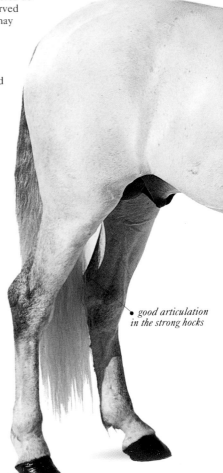

good articulation in the strong hocks

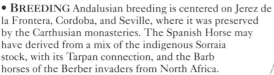

HEIGHT
Stands around 15.2hh.

INFLUENCES

BARB
Passed on fiery, courageous spirit, strength, stamina, and great agility.

SORRAIA
The "primitive" base stock gave hardiness and noted endurance.

Colors Bay, Gray	Uses Saddle

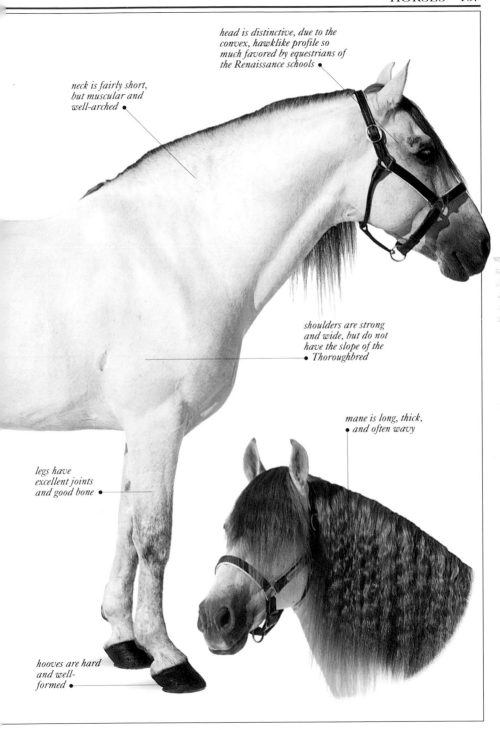

head is distinctive, due to the convex, hawklike profile so much favored by equestrians of the Renaissance schools •

neck is fairly short, but muscular and well-arched •

shoulders are strong and wide, but do not have the slope of the • Thoroughbred

mane is long, thick, • and often wavy

legs have excellent joints and good bone •

hooves are hard and well-formed •

Environment Hot temperate	Origin 16th–17th century	Blood Warm

LUSITANO

The Lusitano is noted as a showy carriage horse as well as a saddle horse of the highest quality, and was once the mount of the Portuguese cavalry. It is the horse most favored by the Portuguese bullfighter and, in that role, is schooled in the advanced movements of the *Haute Ecole*. In more recent years, the Lusitano has become popular outside the Iberian Peninsula and it has an enthusiastic following in both Britain and the United States.

• **BREEDING** The breed is in effect the Portuguese version of the Andalusian (see pp.166–167) and is claimed to be indistinguishable from its neighbor, although it is possible, in some cases, to discern slight differences in type.

• **CHARACTERISTICS** Although sometimes more "on the leg" than the Andalusian, in the eyes of some observers, the intelligent Lusitano is just as brave, quick, and superbly balanced. The naturally elevated action is spectacular, and the breed's agility is remarkable.

PORTUGAL

full tail is well-set into a usually sloping quarter, characterized by length in the hindlegs •

head is fine, with • the distinctive straight, or convex, Spanish profile

Colors All solid, esp. Gray	Uses Saddle, Harness

neck is short and inclined to be thick •

withers are low, rather than sharply defined, but meld into wide shoulders •

• *powerful shoulders*

HEIGHT
Stands between 15 and 16hh.

• *short back and compact body, with well-sprung ribs*

legs are generally long, with considerable length in the cannons below knee and hock •

INFLUENCES

BARB
Passed on fiery, courageous spirit, strength, stamina, and great agility.

SORRAIA
The "primitive" base stock, giving hardiness and endurance.

Environment Hot temperate	Origin 18th century	Blood Warm

ALTER-REAL

As its name suggests, the Alter-Real breed evolved as a horse fit to be the mount of royalty, presenting its rider in the heroic mold, and being ideally suited in spirit and action for classical school riding.

• **BREEDING** The breed was founded in 1748 by the ruling House of Braganza at Vila de Portel in Portugal's Alentejo province, but was moved to Alter in 1756. It started with some 300 of the finest Andalusian mares brought from the area around Jerez de la Frontera, Spain's most famous breeding center. The stud flourished, furnishing horses for the Royal Manège at Lisbon, and the Alter breed became famous for the exhibitions staged there. In the early 19th century, however, much of the stock was lost or stolen when the stud was sacked by Napoleon's troops. In 1834, more disasters overtook Alter, culminating in the abolition of the Royal Stables. A reorganization was attempted under Queen Maria Pia in the late 19th century, and foreign blood was introduced – including English, Norman, Hanoverian, and, most particularly, Arabian. These experiments were unsuccessful and the breed was almost ruined. It was saved by an import of Andalusians. However, the stud archives were largely destroyed after the advent of the Republic in 1910, and it was not until 1932 that constructive efforts were made by the Ministry of Economy to reestablish the breed.

• **CHARACTERISTICS** Despite the vicissitudes it has experienced, the modern Alter, virtually Andalusian again, survives as a highly courageous horse of distinct physical character with an extravagant, high, showy action, especially suited to the *Haute Ecole*.

PORTUGAL: ALTER

tail and mane are thick and luxuriant

INFLUENCE

SPANISH
Gave high courage and distinctive character.

Colors Bay, Brown, Gray	Uses Saddle

HEIGHT
Stands between
15 and 16hh.

strong shoulders and
forearms are positioned
to produce a high,
• animated action

often described as noble,
the head is comparatively
small, with a straight or
• slightly convex profile

body is short and •
compact, and girth
is deep

pasterns are
moderately sloped •

Environment Desert	Origin Prehistoric	Blood Hot

BARB

The Barb is second only to the Arabian as one of the founding breeds of the world's horse population. Its derivative, the Spanish Horse, provided the basis for many of the foremost breeds of Europe and for most of those of the Americas. The Barb must also be recognized as having a part in the evolution of the Thoroughbred.

• **BREEDING** The breed comes from Morocco, in North Africa. It is postulated that it may have constituted a group of wild horses that escaped the effects of the Ice Age. If so, then it is a breed as old as, or older than, the Arabian. At some time, the Barb must have acquired a percentage of Arabian blood, but its conformation owes nothing to the Arabian ideal; this points to the existence of a massively dominant gene. In recent years, there has been much refinement of the traditional Barb, which was the superlative mount of the Berber horsemen who played such a large part in the Muslim Conquest. Although there is no definitive answer to the vexed question of the Barb's origin, it is held that fundamental differences do exist between the Barb and the Arabian.

• **CHARACTERISTICS** Not an impressive horse, the Barb has a sloping quarter, a low-set tail, and a plain head with a skull formation verging on that of the primitive horse types. The profile is straight and sometimes Roman-nosed. Nonetheless, the breed's endurance and stamina are unlimited, and indicative of primitive vigor. It is also exceptionally agile and can travel very fast over short distances.

quarters and hindlegs are far from perfect, but can carry the Barb very fast
• *over short distances*

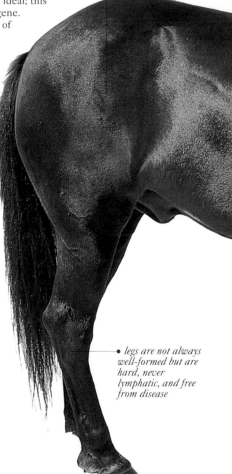

HEIGHT
Stands around 15.2hh.

MOROCCO

• *legs are not always well-formed but are hard, never lymphatic, and free from disease*

Colors All solid	Uses Saddle

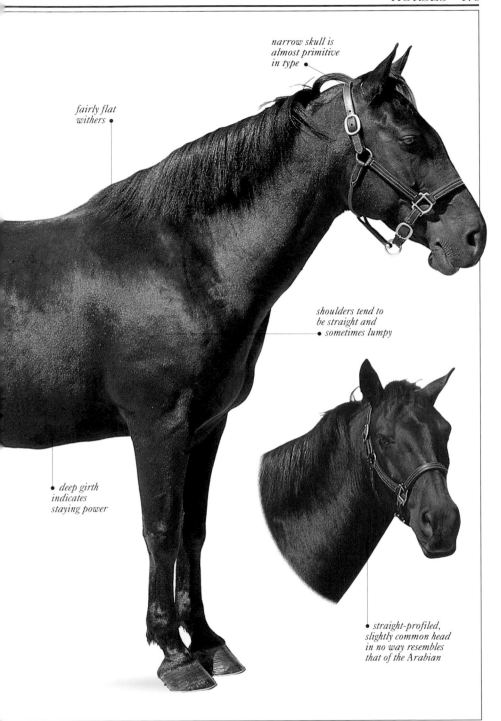

narrow skull is
almost primitive
in type •

fairly flat
withers •

shoulders tend to
be straight and
• sometimes lumpy

• deep girth
indicates
staying power

• straight-profiled,
slightly common head
in no way resembles
that of the Arabian

Environment Desert	Origin Prehistoric	Blood Hot

ARABIAN

The Arabian horse is considered the fountainhead of all the world's breeds and is acknowledged as the principal foundation of the Thoroughbred. It is of the purest descent and is the most ancient of all the equine races.

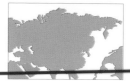

MIDDLE EAST: ARABIAN
PENINSULA

• **BREEDING** A race of horses of Arabian type existed on the Arabian peninsula at least 2,000 years before the Christian era. This is indicated by the existence of art forms and the word-of-mouth evidence handed down by the Bedouin people, who were closely connected with the "desert horse." The prepotent Arabian blood was spread throughout the known world by Muslim conquests initiated by the Prophet Mohammed in the 7th century. As a result, the Arabian became the one essential factor in the development of the world's equines.

• **CHARACTERISTICS** The Arabian horse is the most beautiful of all, at once unmistakable and unforgettable in appearance. The unique outline is governed by the proportions and the skeletal formation. Unlike other breeds, which have 18 ribs, 6 lumbar bones, and 18 tail vertebrae, the Arabian has a 17–5–16 structure. This also accounts for the distinctively high tail carriage. The breed is unsurpassed in stamina; in movement it "floats," and, while it is fiery and courageous, it is innately gentle. The staying power, and the soundness of the breed in respect of wind and leg, make the Arabian an obvious choice for the fast-growing discipline of long-distance, or endurance, riding. Although not nearly so fast as its derivative the Thoroughbred, flat racing confined to Arabians and Anglo-Arabs is also carried on with enthusiasm in many parts of the world. Today, the Arabian is bred extensively throughout the world, with the United States probably having the largest Arabian horse population. All countries breeding Arabian horses have their own studbooks which are approved, in the interests of harmonization, by the World Arabian Horse Organization (WAHO).

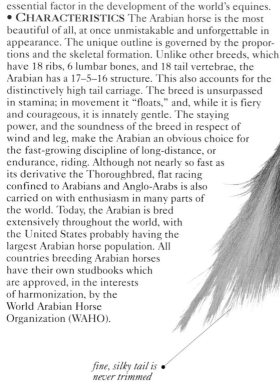

*fine, silky tail is
never trimmed*

*hard, well-formed
feet rarely suffer
from disease*

Colours All solid	Uses Saddle

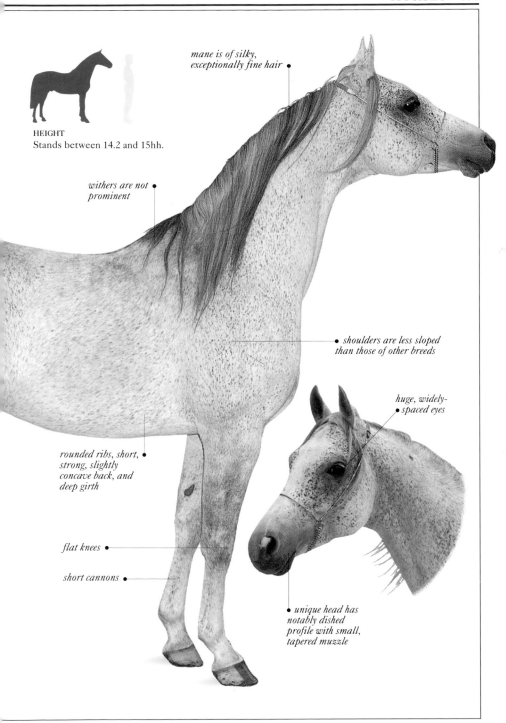

HEIGHT
Stands between 14.2 and 15hh.

mane is of silky,
exceptionally fine hair •

withers are not •
prominent

• shoulders are less sloped
than those of other breeds

huge, widely-
• spaced eyes

rounded ribs, short, •
strong, slightly
concave back, and
deep girth

flat knees •

short cannons •

• unique head has
notably dished
profile with small,
tapered muzzle

Environment Desert	Origin 3,000–2,000 BC	Blood Hot

AKHAL-TEKE

The Akhal-Teke, the world's mystery horse, is the modern equivalent of the Horse Type 3 (see p.11). It epitomizes the thin-skinned, fine-coated, and heat-resistant desert horse, and there could be a relationship between the Akhal-Teke and the Arabian *Munaghi* racing strain. There is evidence that it was in existence over 3,000 years ago in the area of present-day Turkmenistan.

NORTHERN EURASIA:
TURKMENISTAN

• **BREEDING** The Akhal-Teke is bred around the oases of the Karakum Desert, the principal breeding center being at Ashkhabad. It has contributed to many breeds but has been influenced by none. One unsuccessful attempt was made to cross the breed with the Thoroughbred. The Turkomans used the Akhal-Teke for racing, preparing it with great care. It was fed on alfalfa, pellets of mutton fat, eggs, barley, and fried dough cake, and was wrapped in felt as a protection against heat and cold.
• **CHARACTERISTICS** The Akhal-Teke is quite distinctive in appearance, although it hardly conforms to Western ideals of conformation. The metallic, golden-dun coloring is a particular feature. The Akhal-Teke is possessed of boundless stamina and endurance, horses of the breed performing unequaled feats over exceptional distances and in desert conditions. They were able to cover the 2,580 miles (4,152 km) from Ashkhabad to Moscow in 84 days, on minimal rations of feed and water. Today, the Akhal-Teke races, is a long-distance performer, and competes in jumping and dressage.

• *legs are long and slender, with joints set high off the ground*

HEIGHT
Stands around 15.2hh.

INFLUENCE

HORSE TYPE 3
Heat-resistant desert horse of great stamina and endurance.

Colors Metallic Chestnut	Uses Saddle

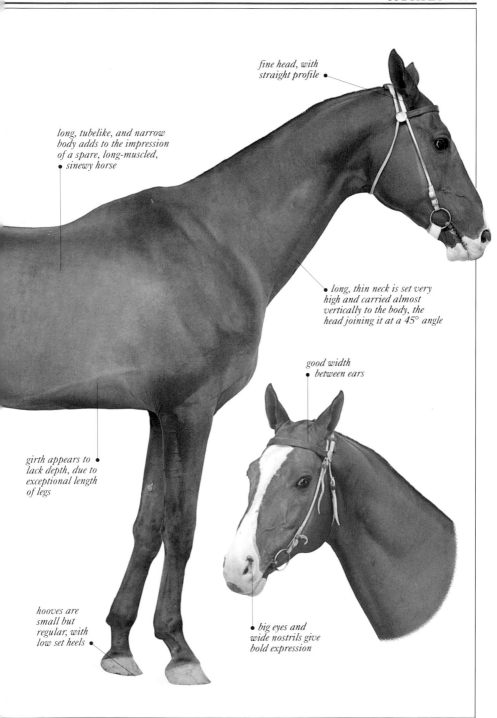

fine head, with straight profile

long, tubelike, and narrow body adds to the impression of a spare, long-muscled, sinewy horse

long, thin neck is set very high and carried almost vertically to the body, the head joining it at a 45° angle

good width between ears

girth appears to lack depth, due to exceptional length of legs

hooves are small but regular, with low set heels

big eyes and wide nostrils give bold expression

Environment Temperate, Controlled	Origin 20th century	Blood Warm

BUDENNY

In the 1920s, the Soviet Union began an ambitious program
of selective breeding, designed to create new, improved breeds.
The process involved experimental crossbreeding using the very
varied native stock. The Budenny, now a kind of universal riding
horse, is an example of the approach taken by the state studs.

NORTHERN EURASIA:
RUSSIAN FEDERATION

• BREEDING Intended as a cavalry horse and named after
Marshal Budenny, the breed, reared in the Rostov region, was
based on Chernomor and Don mares crossed with Thoroughbred
stallions. Kazakh and Kirghiz crosses were also introduced, but
less successfully. Young stock were carefully reared and
performance tested. Three strains were established: Anglo-
Don, Anglo-Don-Chernomor, and Anglo-Chernomor,
which were less numerous. The mares were bred to
the selected Anglo-Don stallions, more
Thoroughbred blood being introduced
as it was thought necessary.

• CHARACTERISTICS The Budenny has a
formidable record as an endurance horse, and
has ability as a jumper and on the track,
where, like many Russian breeds, it is
performance tested. It is a lightly built,
"breedy" horse of acceptable conformation,
but inherits some of the failings of the base
stock, particularly in the legs and joints.
Nonetheless, it is incredibly tough.

hindlegs suffer from
• weak structure

• fine, somewhat oriental
head joins neck gracefully

Colors All solid, esp. Chestnut	Uses Saddle

*neck is light and
straight, corresponding
with overall build* •

*short shoulders,
sometimes inclined
• to be upright*

HEIGHT
Stands around 16hh.

legs, not the •
*best feature, reflect
quality of base stock*

*medium-sized
hooves are quite
well formed* •

INFLUENCES

DON
The base stock
which provided
the tough, hardy
character.

THOROUGHBRED
Contributed size,
better movement
and conformation,
and some quality.

Environment Mountain	Origin 16th century	Blood Warm

KABARDIN

The Kabardin is a mountain horse developed in the northern Caucasus. Like all mountain horses, it is surefooted and agile, and it has an ability to find its way in mist and darkness.

• **BREEDING** The breed evolved in the 16th century as a result of crossing steppe horses with Persian, Turkmene, and Karabakh strains, and has since been improved by selective breeding at state studs. Kabardins, which are used to upgrade neighboring stock, are performance tested on the racetrack. Anglo-Kabardins, the result of crosses with the Thoroughbred, are bigger and faster, but retain much of the hereditary hardiness.

• **CHARACTERISTICS** The breed, in which some natural pacers are found, is noted for its endurance over long distances. Although primarily a saddle horse, the Kabardin is also used in harness.

INFLUENCES

ARABIAN
Upgrading effect gave spirit and greater physical soundness.

TURKMENE
Transmitted desert horse endurance and heat resistance.

KARABAKH
Gave greater speed and agility, and an even temperament.

HEIGHT
Stands between 15 and 15.2hh.

straight shoulders produce an elevated action

hindlegs are sickle-shaped over hocks

NORTHERN EURASIA:
NORTHERN CAUCASUS

Colors Bay, Black	Uses Saddle, Harness

Environment Mountain, Steppe	Origin 17th century	Blood Warm

KARABAKH

The metallic, dun-colored Karabakh is a steppe-mountain horse. It is noted for its speed and ability in mounted games such as *chavgan* (a form of polo) and *surpamakh* (basketball), which are popular in the lands around the Caucasus mountains, and it is also used for a variety of general purposes.

• **BREEDING** Originally a native of the Karabakh mountain areas, the breed was crossed with Persian, Akhal-Teke, and Kabardin horses, and then increasingly with Arabians of the racing strains. It influenced the development of the Don horse in the 18th century. The Karabakh is performance tested on the Baku racetrack in Azerbaijan.

• **CHARACTERISTICS** As well as being fast and agile, it is reputed to be very even-tempered, economical, easily managed, and courageous.

INFLUENCES

AKHAL-TEKE
Contributed to stamina, speed, and excellent resistance to heat.

ARABIAN
Added qualities of refinement, hardiness, and great endurance.

quarters are above average for a steppe breed •

topline is similar to that of a light, elegant riding horse •

HEIGHT
Stands around 14hh.

• girth, like that of the Akhal-Teke, is not notably deep

long, slender • legs

strong, hard • hooves

NORTHERN EURASIA: AZERBAIJAN

Colors Metallic Chestnut, Dun	Uses Saddle

Environment Taiga	Origin 18th century	Blood Warm

ORLOV TROTTER

Before the Revolution, horse breeding in Russia depended on the land owning aristocracy. A notable breeder, Count Alexei Orlov, created the Orlov Trotter at his Khrenov Stud. The Orlov was intended to race, but was also bred as a carriage horse and as an improver of agricultural stock.

• **BREEDING** Orlov began his breeding program in 1778. He used a white Arabian, Smetanka, with a variety of mares. Polkan I, a direct descendant of Smetanka, and out of a Danish mare, was sire of the breed's foundation stallion, Bars I (1784). Bars I, out of a Dutch mare, was mated with Arabian, Dutch, Danish, and English halfbreeds. The required type was obtained by inbreeding to the foundation horse. Systematic performance testing and racing were used to improve the breed. Orlovs were sometimes crossed with Standardbreds to produce Russian Trotters, which were faster but less useful.

• **CHARACTERISTICS** The Orlov is a tall, lightly built horse. It is powerfully muscled and has good general proportions.

NORTHERN EURASIA:
MOSCOW, RUSSIAN
FEDERATION

• *powerful, broad croup and loins*

INFLUENCES

NORFOLK TROTTER
Passed on strong constitution and trotting action.

ARABIAN
Used to refine the somewhat coarse, early agricultural stock.

DUTCH
Contributed its size, substance, and very even temperament.

THOROUGHBRED
Transmitted its physical abilities, improving the action and speed.

Colors Gray, Black, Bay	Uses Harness

HEIGHT
Stands around 16hh.

low withers

*long swan neck set
high on the shoulders*

*long body and
straight back*

*tendency for too-long
legs, a failing inherited
from Dutch mares*

*head is sometimes
coarse, but in most
instances the Arabian
influence is evident*

Environment Steppe	Origin 18th–19th century	Blood Warm

DON

Traditionally, the Don is associated with the Cossack cavalry. Today, it is raced mainly in long-distance events and is far superior to its predecessors. It was much used in the evolution of the Budenny (see pp.178–179).

NORTHERN EURASIA:
RUSSIAN FEDERATION

• **BREEDING** The Don was founded on a mix of tough, steppe-bred Mongolian horses, and swift, heat-resistant Akhal-Tekes and Persian Arabians. Orlovs, Thoroughbreds, and high-class, halfbreed Arabians were used to upgrade the breed in the early 19th century. Since the beginning of the 20th century, there has been little outside influence.

• **CHARACTERISTICS** The Don is a hardy horse that is easily kept and capable of living on the frozen Don steppe. It is adaptable and good-natured, but physically unprepossessing. Although its many conformational deficiencies lead to a restricted, stilted action which is neither elegant nor comfortable, few horses can operate so effectively in conditions of extreme hardship.

croup is rounded and quarters tend to slope away •

• *sickle hocks are often in evidence in hindlegs*

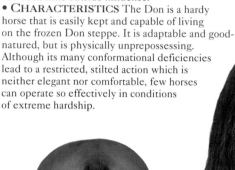

• *hindquarters are generally weak in appearance, if not in reality*

Colors Chestnut, Brown	Uses Saddle, Harness

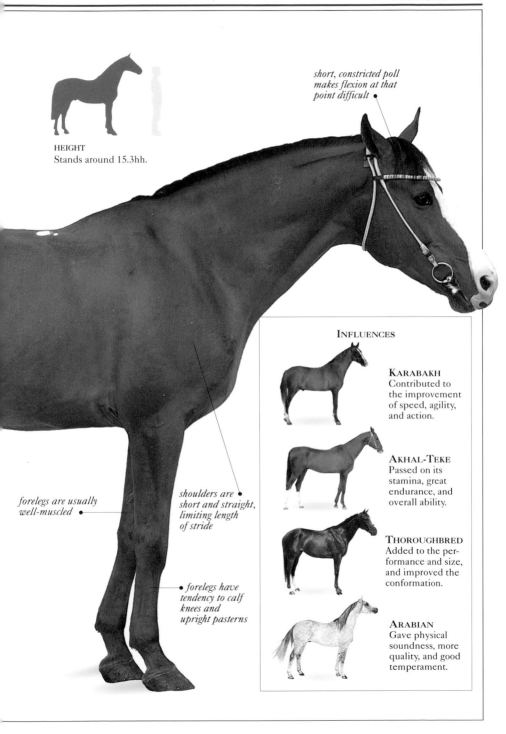

HEIGHT
Stands around 15.3hh.

*short, constricted poll
makes flexion at that
point difficult* •

INFLUENCES

KARABAKH
Contributed to
the improvement
of speed, agility,
and action.

AKHAL-TEKE
Passed on its
stamina, great
endurance, and
overall ability.

THOROUGHBRED
Added to the per-
formance and size,
and improved the
conformation.

ARABIAN
Gave physical
soundness, more
quality, and good
temperament.

*shoulders are
short and straight,
limiting length
of stride* •

*forelegs are usually
well-muscled* •

*• forelegs have
tendency to calf
knees and
upright pasterns*

Environment Steppe, Taiga	Origin Prehistoric	Blood Warm

PRZEWALSKI'S HORSE

In general terms, it is possible to say that modern horse breeds derive from the four "primitive" equine strains that survived the Ice Age – the Tarpan, the Tundra Horse, the Forest Horse, and Przewalski's Horse. Of these, the forest and steppe Tarpan of eastern Europe, *Equus przewalski gmelini antonius*, survives only in a "replica" herd maintained at Popielno in Poland. The Tundra Horse of northeast Siberia, which almost certainly has not contributed to the domestic stock of horses, is extinct, and so, too, is the heavy, slow-moving horse of northern Europe, *Equus przewalski silvaticus*, the Forest or Diluvial Horse. Therefore, the sole survivor of these founding fathers is *Equus przewalski przewalski poliakov*, which is now known as Przewalski's Horse, or the Asian Wild Horse. Though extinct in the wild, it is preserved in zoos and some private stables.

MONGOLIA: TACHIN SCHAH MOUNTAINS

• **BREEDING** This primitive horse is named after a Polish colonel, N.M. Przewalski (1839–1888). He discovered a wild herd in Mongolia in 1881, in the area of the Tachin Schah Mountains (literally, the Mountains of the Yellow Horses), on the edge of the Gobi Desert.

• **CHARACTERISTICS** Przewalski's Horse is fierce and untamed, and has a unique, primitive vigor. It displays characteristics that are not found in the domestic horse – for instance, a chromosome count of 66, as opposed to 64 in the domestic animal. The mane is upright, the body color is sand-dun with black legs, sometimes with zebra stripes, and there is a pronounced dorsal eel stripe.

quarters slope away •

lower half of tail carries coarse, black hair •

HEIGHT
Stands between 12 and 14.2hh.

hooves are very hard, big, flat, and narrow •

Colors Dun	Uses Feral

short, upright mane
is typically primitive •

• profile is straight
or convex

little or no
• forelock

short •
cannons

• head is long and heavy
with small eyes set high,
giving the impression of
even greater length

Environment Tropical	Origin 13th–14th century	Blood Warm

KATHIAWARI

The Kathiawari can be looked upon as being indigenous to the Indian subcontinent. Its homeland is Kathiawari, the peninsula framed by the Gulfs of Kutch and Khamba on India's western coast. It is also found in Gujerat, in southern Rajasthan, and throughout Maharashtra.

INDIA: KATHIAWARI PROVINCE

• **BREEDING** The origin of the distinctive Kathiawari breed lies with the Arabian imports from the Gulf states to the province's principal port of Verval, in the days of the Mongol emperors, and then in later years to Bombay. These horses were crossed with native stock carrying much eastern blood – the Kabuli and Baluchi strains, for example. From that point, the horses were bred selectively by the princely houses. There are 28 distinct strains recognized.

• **CHARACTERISTICS** The tough and hardy Kathiawari is a narrow-built horse, like the Arabian in general appearance. The best examples exhibit the characteristic high tail carriage. Many have a natural ability to pace, indicating an affinity with central Asian breeds. They are claimed to be intelligent, docile, and affectionate.

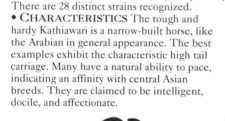

• *quarters appear weak*

• *hindlegs seem to lack strength in comparison with European breeds*

• *very distinctive head, with exceptionally mobile ears which curve inward until tips are touching*

Colors All, except Black	Uses Harness, Saddle

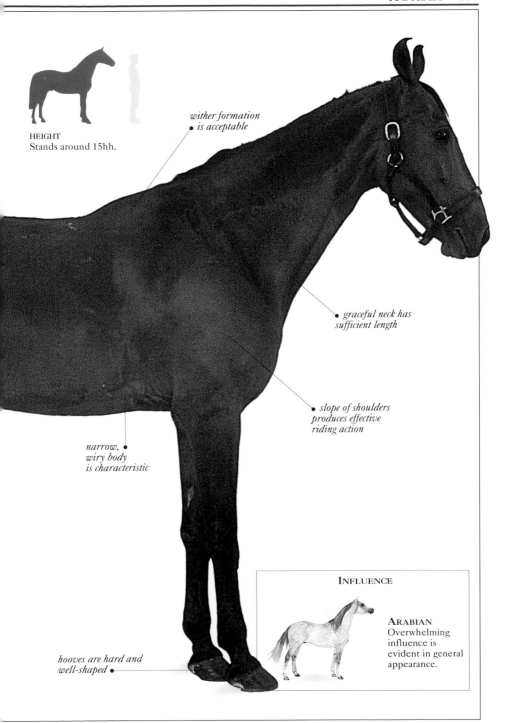

HEIGHT
Stands around 15hh.

*wither formation
is acceptable*

*graceful neck has
sufficient length*

*slope of shoulders
produces effective
riding action*

*narrow,
wiry body
is characteristic*

*hooves are hard and
well-shaped*

INFLUENCE

ARABIAN
Overwhelming
influence is
evident in general
appearance.

Environment Tropical	Origin 19th century	Blood Warm

INDIANBRED

Military requirements in India still call for numbers of cavalry remounts, pack animals, and mules, and the Indianbred, developed specifically to fulfill the modern need for an all-around horse, continues to be produced at army studs and remount depots.

NORTHERN AND CENTRAL INDIA

• **BREEDING** In the early days of the British Raj, Indian cavalry was mounted largely on horses that were predominantly Arabian in origin, troopers under the prevailing system providing their own horses. In the early 1800s, the Kathiawari was in demand, as well as the Kabuli and Baluchi horses. Around the turn of the century, however, large numbers of Walers were imported from Australia, and these became the standard remount for Indian cavalry up to the time the regiments were mechanized. It is from the base provided by these horses, with substantial crosses with the Thoroughbred, that the modern Indianbred troop horse is bred for the mounted formations still in operation.

• **CHARACTERISTICS** The Indianbred horse is of the best trooper type and is not dissimilar to a good stamp of middleweight hunter. It is proportionate and well-made, with good legs and hooves. Outside of military duties, it is often a good, all-around performer in competitive disciplines. The horses are noted for their equable temperament and soundness of constitution.

• hindlegs are workmanlike and correct in their proportions

INFLUENCES

THOROUGHBRED
Refining influence on conformation; it added to the scope, action, and spirit.

WALER
Gave versatility and substance; aided endurance and constitution.

ARABIAN
Endurance and temperament were paramount. Gave soundness.

Colors All solid	Uses Saddle

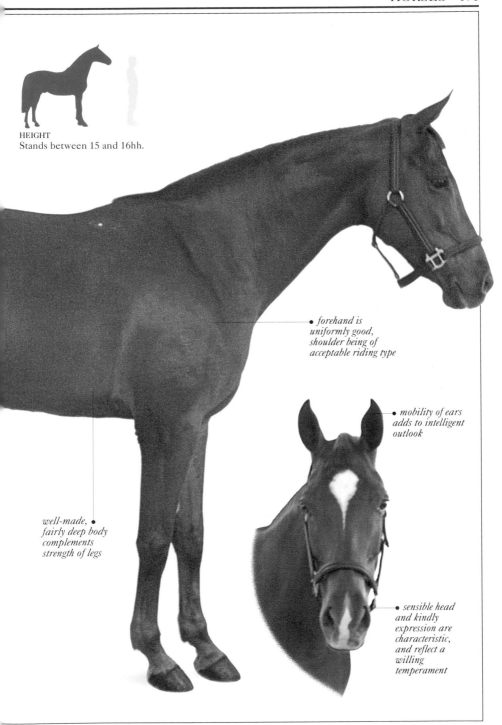

HEIGHT
Stands between 15 and 16hh.

• forehand is
uniformly good,
shoulder being of
acceptable riding type

• mobility of ears
adds to intelligent
outlook

well-made, •
fairly deep body
complements
strength of legs

• sensible head
and kindly
expression are
characteristic,
and reflect a
willing
temperament

Environment Temperate grassland	Origin 19th century	Blood Warm

AUSTRALIAN STOCK HORSE

Horses were first imported to Australia about 200 years ago. They came from South Africa and then increasingly from Europe, and were mainly Arabian and Thoroughbred. The local stock, bred for work on the sheep and cattle stations, came to be known as Walers after the New South Wales province in which they were principally bred.

AUSTRALIA: NEW
SOUTH WALES

• **BREEDING** During World War I, and for some years afterward, as long as there was a military requirement, the Waler was acknowledged as the world's finest cavalry horse. Thousands were employed in Allenby's campaign against the Turks in 1917–1918, and the Indian cavalry regiments were mounted on them before mechanization. From this base was developed what is now called the Australian Stock Horse. It is an Anglo-Arab type, inclining toward the Thoroughbred, and has been influenced by Percheron and pony blood, and also by the Quarter Horse, a breed of increasing popularity in Australia.

• **CHARACTERISTICS** The modern Stock Horse is more Thoroughbred in appearance than the old Waler. It is a superb and very practical all-arounder, with great endurance and stamina. A hard, quality horse, it is exceptionally agile, up to weight, and has an easy disposition. At this time, there is an absence of fixed type and there are no specific standards of conformation.

strong quarters contribute to the agility for which the breed is renowned

HEIGHT
Stands between 15 and 16hh.

hocks are strong, the joints set low to the ground

Colors All solid, mainly Bay	Uses Saddle

strong, well-made back, ideally suited to carry a saddle

head inclines toward the Thoroughbred, but often with a chunkiness suggestive of the Quarter Horse

deep chested, with the good, sloped shoulders of an all-around riding horse

good bone, short cannons, and hard hooves are usual

INFLUENCES

WALER
Gave stamina, versatility, and an equable temperament.

THOROUGHBRED
Added speed and refinement; improved the action and scope.

Environment Cool temperate	Origin 19th century	Blood Warm

AMERICAN SADDLEBRED

The most famous and numerous of the American gaited breeds is the American Saddlebred, formerly called the Kentucky Saddler. It originally evolved in the southern states of America as a practical all-around performer, but is now regarded as a brilliant, if artificial, show ring horse, either under saddle or in harness.

USA: KENTUCKY

• **BREEDING** The American Saddlebred was developed from the old Narragansett Pacer, workhorse of the Rhode Island plantations, and the Canadian Pacer – both naturally gaited breeds. The breed was refined and acquired its impressive, eye-catching appearance, speed, and brilliance of movement through the introduction of Morgan and Thoroughbred blood.

• **CHARACTERISTICS** An imposing horse with great presence and spirit, the Saddlebred performs the walk, trot, and canter with a high, elevated action (three-gaited). The additional paces, exhibited by a five-gaited horse, are the four-beat, prancing "slow gait" and the breathtaking, full-speed "rack." When its hooves are trimmed normally, the Saddlebred can be used for pleasure and for trail riding.

quarters have a level croup, with the tail set high and nicked to emphasize carriage •

• legs are light and elegant

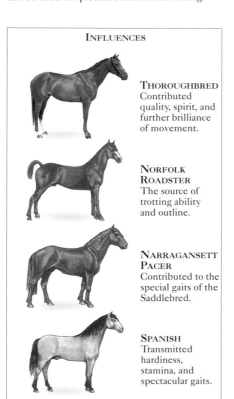

INFLUENCES

THOROUGHBRED
Contributed quality, spirit, and further brilliance of movement.

NORFOLK ROADSTER
The source of trotting ability and outline.

NARRAGANSETT PACER
Contributed to the special gaits of the Saddlebred.

SPANISH
Transmitted hardiness, stamina, and spectacular gaits.

Colors All solid	Uses Show, Pleasure, Saddle, Harness

HEIGHT
Stands between 15 and 16hh.

neck is set high into
shoulders, adding to
• elevated carriage

quality head is finely
drawn, with neat,
sharp ears, breadth
between the bold eyes,
a small muzzle, and
• wide, open nostrils

trunk is typical of the •
horse's elegant outline
and is wonderfully
sprung through the ribs

sloping pasterns
provide a comfortable,
springy ride •

hooves are usually
grown long, especially
in front, and are shod
with heavy shoes •

Environment Cool temperate	Origin 18th century	Blood Warm

APPALOOSA

The spotted gene in horses is as old as the equine race, but the credit for the development of a distinctive spotted breed, the Appaloosa, has to be given to the Nez Percé Indians of North America who lived in the Pacific Northwest. Their lands included the valley of the Palouse River after which the horses were named.

USA: OREGON

• **BREEDING** The breed developed in the 18th century, and was founded on the Spanish stock brought to the Americas, which included a number of spotted strains. The Nez Percé, who were skillful horse breeders, practiced strict selection policies. The result of their care was an unmistakable workhorse which was attractively colored and essentially practical. In 1877, the tribe and its horses were almost exterminated as United States troops seized the tribal lands. However, the breed was revived in 1938 when the Appaloosa Horse Club was formed in Moscow, Idaho. Its registry is now the third largest in the world.

• **CHARACTERISTICS** The present-day Appaloosa is a stock and pleasure horse that is used increasingly for jumping and racing. It is noted for its endurance, stamina, and good temperament. There are five recognized Appaloosa coat patterns: blanket, marble, leopard, snowflake, and frost (see pp.22–23).

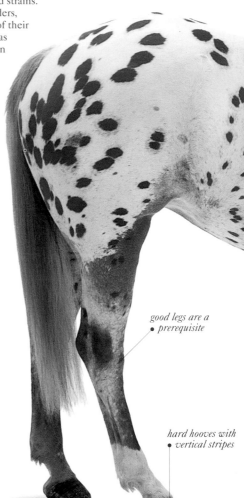

good legs are a • prerequisite

hard hooves with • vertical stripes

HEIGHT
Stands between 14.2 and 15.2hh.

INFLUENCE

SPANISH
Added strength, adaptability, hardiness, and the spotted coat.

Colors Spotted	Uses Saddle

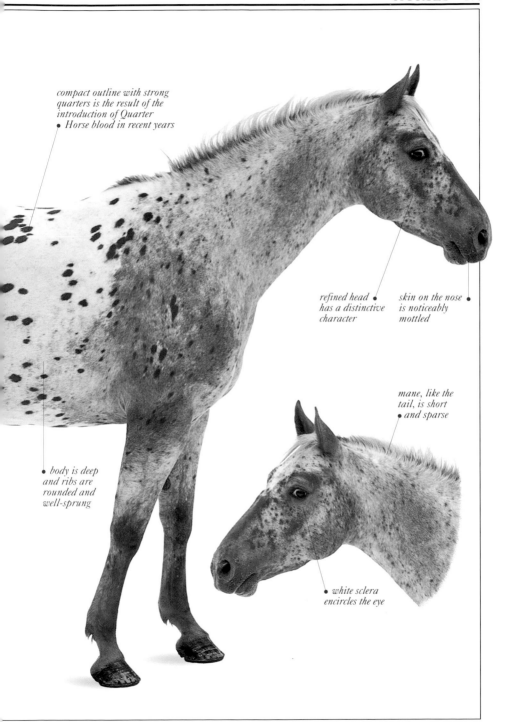

compact outline with strong
quarters is the result of the
introduction of Quarter
• Horse blood in recent years

refined head •
has a distinctive
character

skin on the nose •
is noticeably
mottled

mane, like the
tail, is short
• and sparse

• body is deep
and ribs are
rounded and
well-sprung

• white sclera
encircles the eye

Environment Cool temperate	Origin 19th century	Blood Warm

MISSOURI FOX TROTTER

The Missouri Fox Trotter is an American gaited breed like
the Tennessee Walker and the Saddlebred. It was established
in the Ozark Mountains in Arkansas and Missouri, about 1820,
as a utility horse suited to the country and the needs of the
settlers. A studbook for the breed was opened in 1948. The
modern Fox Trotter is an all-around pleasure and show horse.
It is usually ridden in western tack. The gaits evolved
naturally, and artificial aids are banned by the breed society.

USA: ARKANSAS AND MISSOURI

• **BREEDING** The early American settlers interbred
Morgans, Thoroughbreds, and horses of the initial Spanish-
Barb ancestry. They then introduced Saddlebred and
Tennessee Walking Horse blood to create a plain, compact
horse of easy temperament, that was distinguished by a
smooth, peculiarly broken gait that could be
maintained, over long distances and rough
ground, at a regular speed of 5 mph (8 km/h).
• **CHARACTERISTICS** The most
notable characteristic is the comfortable,
surefooted, sliding gait that produces
very little movement in the back.
The horse walks with spirited
action in front while trotting with
the hindlegs. The hind hooves
reach well forward and touch
down with a sliding movement.
Over short distances, the
famous Fox Trot gait produces
speeds of 10 mph (16 km/h).

*although inclined to be
plain, the head is neat and
intelligent, without coarse
fleshiness, and has pointed
and mobile ears* •

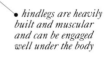

• *hindlegs are heavily
built and muscular
and can be engaged
well under the body*

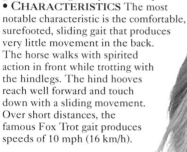

Colors All, primarily Chestnut	Uses Saddle

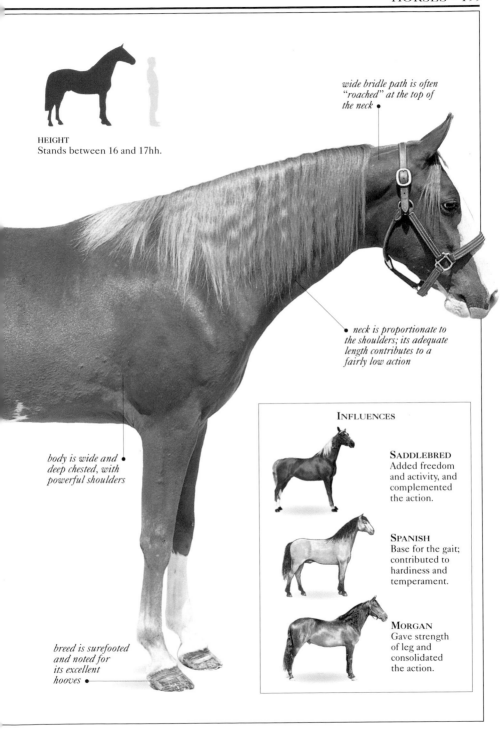

HEIGHT
Stands between 16 and 17hh.

wide bridle path is often "roached" at the top of the neck •

• neck is proportionate to the shoulders; its adequate length contributes to a fairly low action

body is wide and • deep chested, with powerful shoulders

breed is surefooted and noted for its excellent hooves •

INFLUENCES

SADDLEBRED
Added freedom and activity, and complemented the action.

SPANISH
Base for the gait; contributed to hardiness and temperament.

MORGAN
Gave strength of leg and consolidated the action.

Environment Temperate, Controlled	Origin 18th century	Blood Warm

MORGAN

The Morgan is unusual in that it descends from one prepotent stallion, Justin Morgan. It is a versatile pleasure horse, whether ridden western or English style, and is increasingly a show horse, competing in park classes either under saddle or in harness. Until mechanization, the Morgan was the chosen remount of the United States Army. A statue of Justin Morgan, at the Morgan Horse Farm at the University of Vermont, is a permanent memorial to one of the world's most extraordinary horses.

USA: MASSACHUSETTS AND VERMONT

• **BREEDING** The founder of the breed was born in either 1789 or 1793 at West Springfield, Massachusetts. In 1795, he was acquired by a Vermont schoolmaster, Justin Morgan, and was named after him. He was worked hard at the plow, hauling timber, and clearing woodland. He was matched in severe weight-pulling contests and raced in harness and under saddle, but was never beaten. Also a most prolific and potent sire, all Morgans relate back to him, although his own breeding has never been established. It has been suggested that he was sired by an early Thoroughbred, True Briton. Another theory attributes the horse to a Friesian import, and the Welsh claim him as the progeny of a Welsh Cob – which is not impossible.

• **CHARACTERISTICS** The park Morgan is deliberately shod to produce an artificially elevated action. However, if the hooves are trimmed normally, the horse moves freely at the basic gaits, without undue knee lift. The breed is hardy and possessed of great stamina and exceptional strength. More refined in appearance than the earlier and more chunky type, today's Morgan is spirited, but intelligent and easily managed.

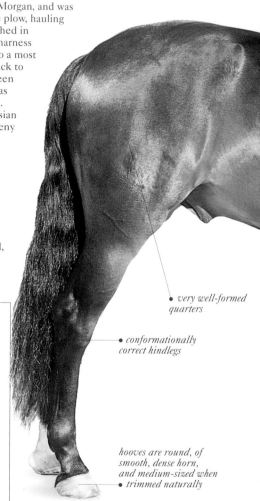

• *very well-formed quarters*

• *conformationally correct hindlegs*

hooves are round, of smooth, dense horn, and medium-sized when • *trimmed naturally*

INFLUENCES

ARABIAN
The Arabian was a possible, but unsubstantiated, influence.

THOROUGHBRED
Early Thoroughbred blood may have been an influence.

Colors All solid, except Gray	Uses Saddle, Harness

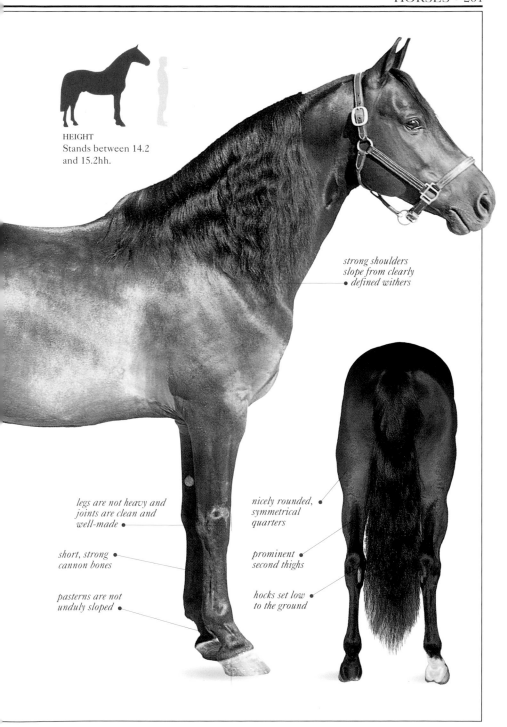

HEIGHT
Stands between 14.2
and 15.2hh.

strong shoulders
slope from clearly
defined withers

legs are not heavy and
joints are clean and
well-made

short, strong
cannon bones

pasterns are not
unduly sloped

nicely rounded,
symmetrical
quarters

prominent
second thighs

hocks set low
to the ground

Environment Desert, Savanna	Origin 16th–17th century	Blood Warm

MUSTANG

The name "mustang" is a corruption of the Spanish *mesteña*, meaning a group or herd of horses. At the beginning of the 20th century, there were about one million wild horses in the western United States. By 1970, the herds were devastated when they were hunted to provide grazing land for cattle and sheep ranchers. They are now protected by law.

• **BREEDING** The Mustang herds originated from the horses that were brought to America by the Spanish in the 16th century. The Spanish established cattle ranches in Mexico, and horses that were turned loose or strayed eventually became feral, forming the nucleus of the herds that spread upward into North America and the western plains.

• **CHARACTERISTICS** Mustangs are agile, hardy, and often very fast. Although they often degenerate into poor quality scrub stock, they frequently retain the strength and some of the appearance of their Spanish forebears. Mustangs provided the base for stock such as the legendary Chickasaw Indian Pony, which influenced the Quarter Horse.

INFLUENCE

SPANISH Responsible for wiry strength, speed, and hardy constitution.

head in this good specimen is essentially Spanish in character •

luxuriant mane and tail, and body coloring are typical of the Spanish horse •

• *body is strong and broad but without prominence in withers*

• *hard and enduring legs*

hooves do not need • *shoes*

HEIGHT
Stands between 13.2 and 15hh.

USA: WESTERN STATES

Colors All	Uses Feral

Environment Hot temperate	Origin 15th–16th century	Blood Warm

PALOMINO

The ancient golden palomino coloring occurs in a variety of horses and ponies as well as established breeds. The Palomino is, therefore, a "color type" and not a "breed" in the accepted sense. The Spanish brought palomino coloring to America, where it now occurs in the Quarter Horse and the Saddlebred. The name may derive from a Spanish don, Juan de Palomino, or a golden Spanish grape.

• **BREEDING** Although not strictly a breed, Palomino horses are bred extensively in the USA. The American Palomino Horse Association registers horses meeting specific standards and measuring between 14.1 and 16hh. For registration, one parent must be registered, and the other parent must be Quarter Horse, Arabian, or Thoroughbred.

• **CHARACTERISTICS** These depend on the dominant genetic influence. The most favored cross to produce palomino is chestnut with palomino, or chestnut with cream or albino.

INFLUENCE

SPANISH
Passed on many physical attributes, and also the distinctive color.

USA

mane and tail are silvery white and should not contain more than 15 percent dark hair

color is that of a newly minted gold coin, or three shades lighter or darker

if white markings occur on legs, they must not extend above knees or hocks

HEIGHT
Any height is acceptable.

Colors Palomino	Uses Saddle

Environment Savanna	Origin 16th century	Blood Warm

PINTO, OR PAINT HORSE

The Pinto Horse Association and the American Paint Horse Association, both with their headquarters in Fort Worth, Texas, both register part-colored equines. The Pinto Horse Association registers any breed of horse or pony that meets its color requirement, dividing them into stock type, hunter, pleasure type, and saddle type. It has a similar classification for ponies. The American Paint Horse Association registers the offspring of horses with Paint, Quarter Horse, and Thoroughbred registration papers.

USA

• **BREEDING** Pintos and Paints are descendants of the Spanish horses brought to America in the 16th century. Until the 18th and 19th centuries, a part-colored strain was evident in Europe, in horses derived from Spanish blood. The name "Pinto" comes from the Spanish word *pintado*, meaning "painted," and in the vernacular of the western cowboy this became "paint." Part-colored horses, or even spotted ones, were also called calicos.

• **CHARACTERISTICS** There are two types of coloring: ovaro and tobiano. Ovaro is a basic solid coat with large, irregular splashes of white over it. Tobiano is a white base coat with large, irregular patches of solid color. It is difficult to accord the Pinto breed status, in the accepted meaning of the word, because of the lack of consistency in type and size.

• strong quarters

good legs and hooves are sought – most part-colored horses fulfill • this requirement

HEIGHT
Stands between 15 and 16hh.

INFLUENCE

SPANISH
Gave physical attributes as well as the colored coat patterns.

Colors Part	Uses Saddle

inclining toward a stock-
horse type, the build of this
• Pinto is powerful

forehand of this specimen is
• of exemplary riding type

this type of •
coloring is
called "ovaro"

sensible, quality •
head of this particular
Pinto reflects underlying
Thoroughbred influence

Environment Cool temperate	Origin 18th–19th century	Blood Warm

QUARTER HORSE

The Quarter Horse, the first all-American breed, is claimed to be "the most popular horse in the world." Over 3 million are registered with the American Quarter Horse Association.

• **BREEDING** Its foundation was English horses, imported to Virginia about 1611, and Spanish stock, brought to America in the previous century. It was used for every sort of work: farming, hauling, working cattle, in harness, and under saddle. The settlers raced them over stretches of about a quarter of a mile, hence the name Quarter Horse, from the horse's ability to sprint faster than any other breed over this distance. In the West, it is the supreme pony, working cattle with an uncanny instinct.

• **CHARACTERISTICS** The old Quarter Horse was noted for massive quarters that facilitated its sprinting ability from a standing start. The recent infusion of Thoroughbred blood, with the aim of increasing racing speed, has tended to reduce this notable characteristic.

USA

• *hips are wide and legs are heavily muscled in thighs and gaskins*

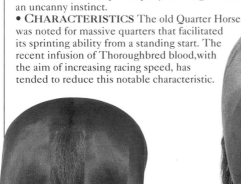

• *to accentuate its quarters, the horse is often photographed from behind*

Colors All solid	Uses Saddle

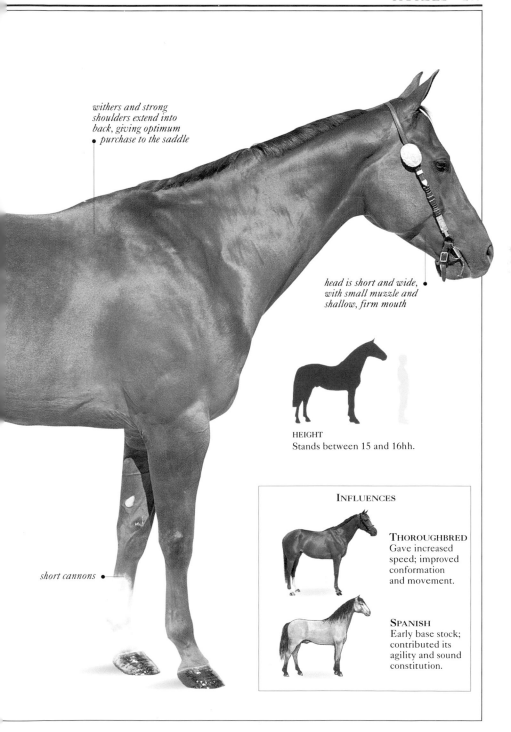

withers and strong
shoulders extend into
back, giving optimum
• purchase to the saddle

head is short and wide, •
with small muzzle and
shallow, firm mouth

HEIGHT
Stands between 15 and 16hh.

short cannons •

INFLUENCES

THOROUGHBRED
Gave increased
speed; improved
conformation
and movement.

SPANISH
Early base stock;
contributed its
agility and sound
constitution.

Environment Cool temperate	Origin 18th–19th century	Blood Warm

TENNESSEE WALKING HORSE

"If you ride one today, you'll own one tomorrow," says the Tennessee Walking Horse Breeders' and Exhibitors' Association. The modern Walker is one of the unique group of American gaited horses developed in the 19th century. Originally ridden by the plantation owner, today's Walker is a popular family horse.

• **BREEDING** The Walker derives from the old Narragansett Pacer and evolved as a mix of Standardbred, Morgan, Thoroughbred, and American Saddlebred. The foundation sire is the Standardbred trotter, Black Allan, whose peculiar walk was inherited by his progeny.

• **CHARACTERISTICS** The Walker has three "bounce-free" gaits: a flat walk; a running walk, which has four beats and in which the head nods in time and the teeth click; and a high, smooth, rocking-chair canter. The breed is said to be the most naturally good-tempered of all equines.

INFLUENCES

NARRAGANSETT PACER Provided the original, natural pacing gait.

THOROUGHBRED Introduced additional refinement; improved conformation.

STANDARDBRED Gave the peculiar walk through the foundation sire, Black Allan.

short-coupled body with barrel having • square appearance

HEIGHT Stands between 15 and 16hh.

USA: TENNESSEE

Colors All solid	Uses Saddle

Environment Cool temperate	Origin 19th century	Blood Warm

STANDARDBRED

In many countries harness racing is more popular than flat racing. In America, it has a following of over 30 million people. The Standardbred is the supreme harness racer. It can cover 1 mile (1.6 km) in 1 minute 55 seconds. The breed got its name in 1879, when a speed standard was set for entry into the register.

• **BREEDING** The Standardbred was based on the English Thoroughbred, Messenger, a horse with strong Norfolk Trotter connections, who was imported in 1788. The foundation sire was Messenger's descendant, Hambletonian 10, foaled in 1849. Between 1851 and 1875, this horse sired 1,335 offspring. Hambletonian's peculiar and high-crouped conformation contributed to his success as a sire of harness racers.

• **CHARACTERISTICS** Standardbreds either trot conventionally or pace, employing the lateral, swaying gait. Pacers are faster and less likely to break the gait, and are preferred in America. In Europe, trotters are more numerous. Both have iron hard legs and good hooves.

INFLUENCES

THOROUGHBRED Added speed, and improved straightness of action and conformation.

NARRAGANSETT PACER Provided the basis for a natural pacing gait.

MORGAN Transmitted robust constitution, endurance, and stamina.

croup is usually higher than withers – giving enormous propulsive thrust to quarters

HEIGHT Stands around 15.2hh.

USA: EASTERN SEABOARD

Colors Bay, Brown, Chestnut	Uses Harness

Environment Cool temperate	Origin 19th century	Blood Warm

COLORADO RANGER

Besides the Appaloosa, another American spotted
breed of interest is the Colorado Ranger, otherwise called
the Rangerbred. This breed has records dating from 1878
and incorporates some illustrious bloodlines. It is less well-
known than the Appaloosa because, up to 1968,
membership of the Colorado Ranger Horse Association,
Inc. was limited to 50 persons.

USA: COLORADO

• **BREEDING** The Colorado Ranger was founded on two
horses presented to General Ulysses Grant by Sultan Abdul
Hamid II of Turkey in 1878. They were the purebred gray
Arabian called Leopard, and a Barb stallion called Linden
Tree. Since then, crosses have been made with
Thoroughbreds and Quarter Horses.

• **CHARACTERISTICS** The lines established by the
Colorado breeders produced excellent working
horses of a particular refinement. Most Rangers
have a patterned coat, but it is their pedigree that
is the prime requirement for registration.

*symmetry and •
strength in
hindquarters are
necessary in a
working horse*

*• good, sound
legs*

*well-made,
• hard hooves*

Colors Spotted	Uses Saddle

HEIGHT
Stands around 15.2hh.

head has pleasing
proportions and an
intelligent outlook

body is compact
and deep, but not
heavy – evidence of
Arabian/Barb
ancestry remains

INFLUENCES

ARABIAN
Contributed to
the symmetry of
form; transmitted
prepotency.

BARB
Complemented
the Arabian
qualities and
added increased
agility.

SPANISH
This sound and
hardy breed
provided the
base stock.

Environment Savanna	Origin 16th century	Blood Warm

CRIOLLO

Although the Criollo is the native horse of
Argentina, it appears in slightly different forms
and under a variety of names all over the South
American continent. For instance, in Brazil, it
is the *Crioulo Brazileiro*. In Argentina, the
Criollo is the indispensable mount of the
gaucho, the cowboy of the Pampas, and has
played an important part in the evolution of
the famous Argentinian polo pony.

• **BREEDING** The Criollo originated from
the Spanish stock brought to South America in
the 16th century. These horses carried much
enduring Barb blood. The first significant
imports were made in 1535 by Don Pedro
Mendoza, the founder of Buenos Aires.
Later, when the city had been sacked by the
Indians, these horses ran wild over large areas
of the country and bred freely.

• **CHARACTERISTICS** The Criollo is
probably the toughest, soundest horse in the
world, a tribute to its Spanish ancestry. It is
capable of living in climatic extremes on
minimal feed, has incredible powers of
endurance, and is noted for its longevity.

INFLUENCE

SPANISH
Contributed to
phenomenal
toughness and
endurance.

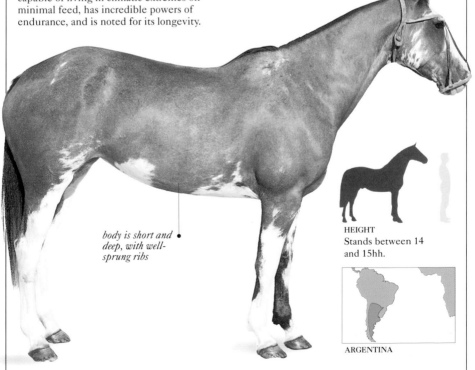

*medium-sized head is
sometimes convex in
profile, denoting
Spanish origin*

*body is short and
deep, with well-
sprung ribs*

HEIGHT
Stands between 14
and 15hh.

ARGENTINA

Colors Predominantly Dun	Uses Saddle

Environment Savanna	Origin 16th century	Blood Warm

PASO

The Peruvian Paso, or stepping horse, shares a common ancestry with the Criollo. It is distinguished by its unique lateral gait and a particular conformation, confirmed by selective breeding over three centuries or more.

• **BREEDING** Breeding is directed at perfecting the natural gait – the paso. The action involves a vigorous, round movement of the forelegs, supported by powerful use of the hindlegs, the quarters being held low. This can be kept up for long periods over rough country.

• **CHARACTERISTICS** The breed is very tough. The hindlegs and hind pasterns are long, and the joints are unusually flexible overall. These factors contribute to the comfort of the paso gait.

INFLUENCE

SPANISH
Early Spanish gaited strains were responsible for paso action.

PERU

HEIGHT
Stands between 14 and 15hh.

• *chest is broad and deep, and musculature is very well-developed*

great depth in body, • *allowing room for unusually large lungs*

Colors All solid	Uses Saddle

HEAVY HORSES

Environment Taiga	Origin 19th century	Blood Cold

NORTH SWEDISH HORSE

The attractive North Swedish Horse is a close relation of
Norway's Døle Gudbrandsdal, and at one time was much
influenced by that breed. It is a small, compact, and very
active draft horse much used in forestry, at which it excels,
and in agriculture. The lighter Døle crosses (which share
the studbook) are specialist harness racers.

• **BREEDING** The principal stud is at Wangen. From
early this century, stringent performance testing has been
in force. The horses are subject to log-hauling tests, and
their pulling power is measured against an ergometer.
Mature animals undergo further draft tests, and all
stock have hooves and legs checked radiologically.

• **CHARACTERISTICS** The horses are noted for
their good temperament, freedom of action, courage,
and strength. The breed is exceptionally long-lived
and appears immune to most common diseases.

SWEDEN: NORTH

*croup slopes
noticeably*

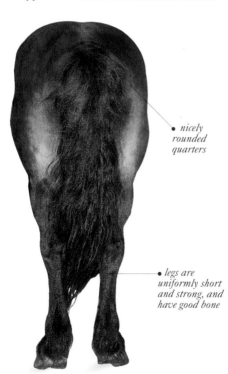

*nicely
rounded
quarters*

*legs are
uniformly short
and strong, and
have good bone*

Colors All solid	Uses Light Draft

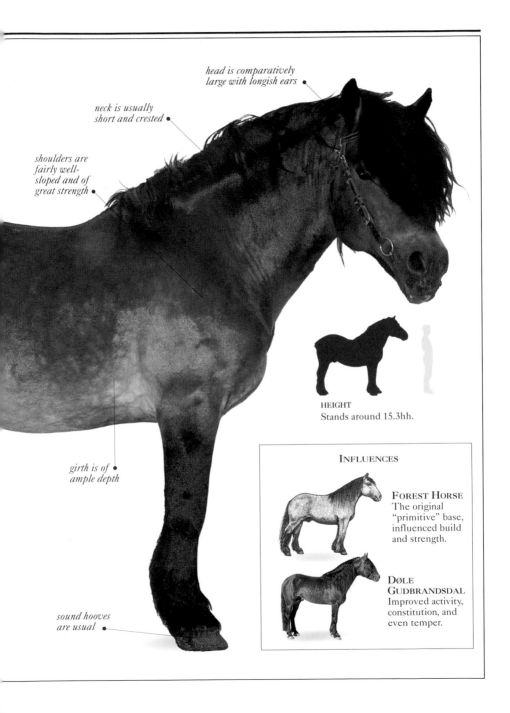

head is comparatively
large with longish ears •

neck is usually
short and crested •

shoulders are
fairly well-
sloped and of
great strength •

girth is of •
ample depth

sound hooves
are usual •

HEIGHT
Stands around 15.3hh.

INFLUENCES

FOREST HORSE
The original
"primitive" base,
influenced build
and strength.

DØLE
GUDBRANDSDAL
Improved activity,
constitution, and
even temper.

Environment Temperate, Controlled	Origin 12th century	Blood Cold

JUTLAND

The Jutland, Denmark's own breed of heavy horse, has been bred on the Jutland Peninsula since the Middle Ages and before. It was used for agriculture and all types of draft but today, when its numbers have declined, it is most often seen hauling brewers' drays on city streets in Europe.

• **BREEDING** Like other heavy horse breeds, the Jutland is derived from the coldblood Forest Horse of prehistory. By the 12th century, it had been developed as a sturdy warhorse, up to weight, enduring, and economical to keep. In the 19th century, the modern Jutland began to take shape. This was as a result of crosses to the Cleveland Bay and the Yorkshire Coach Horse; however, the overwhelming influence is that of the Suffolk Punch, which it resembles so closely, through Oppenheim LXII, imported in 1860. The most important bloodline is that of his descendant, Oldrup Munkedal. The Jutland is largely responsible for the neighboring Schleswig horse, and crosses were still being made well into the 20th century.

• **CHARACTERISTICS** The Jutland is a medium-sized draft horse with a quick, free action. Like that of the Suffolk Punch, the coat is almost always chestnut with a flaxen mane and tail, and the breed's connection with the Suffolk is evident in the compact, round body, the deep girth, and the massive quarters. In one respect, it differs entirely from the Suffolk Punch, for the Jutland's legs carry a heavy feather that is not found in the former. The breed has a reputation for being docile, kindly, and a tireless, willing worker.

DENMARK: JUTLAND PENINSULA

joints are inclined to be round and fleshy

HEIGHT
Stands between 15 and 16hh.

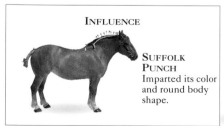

INFLUENCE

SUFFOLK PUNCH
Imparted its color and round body shape.

Colors Chestnut, Roan	Uses Draft

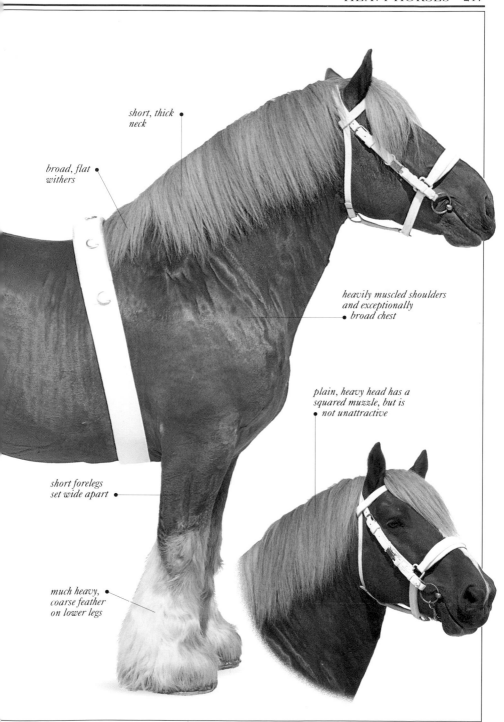

short, thick
neck

broad, flat
withers

heavily muscled shoulders
and exceptionally
broad chest

plain, heavy head has a
squared muzzle, but is
not unattractive

short forelegs
set wide apart

much heavy,
coarse feather
on lower legs

Environment Cool temperate	Origin 1st–2nd century AD	Blood Cold

BRABANT

The Brabant, also known as the Belgian Heavy Draft or *race de trait Belge*, takes its name from one of the breed's principal breeding areas. Although no longer well-known outside its native country, it is one of the most important heavy horse breeds, and has a strong following in the USA.

• **BREEDING** The breed is very old and is thought to descend directly from the Forest or Diluvial horse (*Equus przewalski silvaticus*). Horses like this were known to the Romans, and from the 11th to the 16th centuries, heavy warhorses were produced in Brabant and Flanders. Flanders horses had a profound influence in Europe. For example, in Britain, they were a foundation for Shires and Clydesdales, and may have contributed to the Suffolk Punch. Belgian breeders used established bloodlines to produce a horse that was suited to their climate, types of soil, and economic and social conditions. They resisted the inclusion of foreign blood, practiced a policy of stringent selection, and inbred where it was necessary to preserve exceptional qualities.

• **CHARACTERISTICS** The three principal lines, established in the 19th century, are: *Gros de la Dendre*, founded by Orange 1 and noted for massive bay horses; *Gris du Hainaut*, founded by the stallion Bayard, which has gray, dun, and the distinctive red roan coloring; the third, founded on Jean 1, is the *Colosses de la Mehaique*, which has exceptionally good legs and tremendous strength in the back and loins.

BELGIUM: BRABANT AND FLANDERS

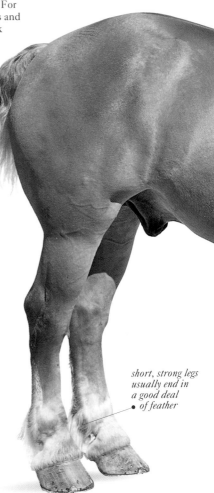

short, strong legs usually end in a good deal • of feather

HEIGHT
Stands between 16.2 and 17hh.

INFLUENCE

FLANDERS HORSE
Gave strength, size, weight, and coat colorings.

Colors Roan, Chestnut	Uses Heavy Draft

square and somewhat
plain head is neat and
relatively small •

back runs into
characteristically
"double-muscled"
croup and massive,
• rounded quarters

short, thick, and powerful neck
is in proportion to enormous
strength of shoulders and
• notably deep barrel

body is very •
compact and
thickset

expression is kind •
and intelligent

Environment Cool temperate	Origin 16th century	Blood Cold

NORIKER

The Noriker is one of Europe's ancient coldblood breeds. It derives its name from the state of Noricum, a vassal province of the Roman Empire corresponding to present-day Austria. Noricum was adjacent to the lands of the horse-raising Venetii, which were to become the home of the Haflinger. There is, therefore, a natural connection between the two breeds. The modern Noriker is still exceptionally popular in Austria and is the established all-purpose workhorse of the central Alps region. Now a breed of fixed and clearly recognizable type, the Noriker is subject to strictly enforced breed standards, and there is a rigorous system of inspection and performance testing.

AUSTRIA AND THE CENTRAL ALPS

• **BREEDING** The early ancestors of the breed developed by the Romans were heavy warhorses, which could also be used in draft and under pack. The Noriker was recognized as a breed from about 1565, when it was taken under the wing of the monasteries and the Salzburg studbook, initiated by the Prince-Archbishop of Salzburg. Heavy Burgundian horses were used to increase the size of the stock, but more important was the introduction of the all-pervasive Spanish blood. Spotted horses, Pinzgauer-Noriker, appeared and these still occur. The Spanish legacy is still evident in a number of other distinctive coat patterns.

• **CHARACTERISTICS** This is a hard, powerful, medium-sized workhorse. The conformational standards stipulate 8½–9½ in (20–24 cm) of bone, short legs of exceptional strength, and a girth measurement of not less than 60 percent of the height at the withers. The breed is hardy, inherently sound, economical, and easily managed.

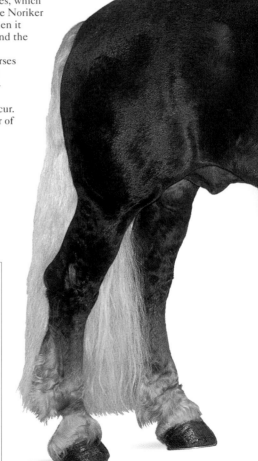

INFLUENCES

SPANISH
Contributed to refinement and to freedom of action.

FOREST HORSE
Primitive base stock gave increased size.

Colors Brown, Black, Chestnut	Uses Light Draft

HEIGHT
Stands between 16 and 17hh.

*alert ears are
placed high •*

*head is defined and never
lymphatic, and nostrils
• are noticeably wide*

*exceptional depth at the •
girth of the broad, compact
body is a requirement of
the breed standard*

*strong, straight legs •
with ample bone and
long, sure action*

Environment Cool temperate	Origin Pre-Christian	Blood Cold

ARDENNAIS

The heavily boned, snub-nosed heavy horses of the Ardennes region of France and Belgium are among the oldest in the world. They were developed during the 19th century to fulfill a variety of requirements, and two types evolved – the lively, light draft type and the slower, but very powerful heavy type, which was the workhorse of northern France.

• **BREEDING** The Ardennes horses developed into specific types by various crosses. Arabian, Thoroughbred, Percheron, and Boulonnais produced the now rare, light, harness type; the bigger Ardennes du Nord was derived from crosses with the Brabant, as was the larger and very powerful Burgundy horse, the Auxois.

• **CHARACTERISTICS** This docile and easily handled breed is naturally hardy due to its harsh environment. Although still used in agriculture, it is also bred for meat.

INFLUENCE

FOREST HORSE The source of the size, weight, and docile temperament.

HEIGHT
Stands around 15.3hh.

compact body, with very short back and exceptional breadth over loins •

straight profiled head has low forehead and prominent eye sockets •

legs are massive and covered with heavy, coarse feathering •

FRANCE: ARDENNES, AND
BELGIUM: SOUTHEAST

Colors Roan	Uses Heavy Draft

Environment Cool temperate	Origin 1st–2nd century AD	Blood Cold

BOULONNAIS

The pronounced oriental influence in the
Boulonnais breed has produced a draft
horse of singular beauty and refinement.
• **BREEDING** The Boulonnais is a native of
northwest France, where there was a special
breed of heavy horses in pre-Christian times.
Eastern horses were first introduced by the
Romans in the first century AD. In the 14th
century, the Boulonnais was used as a warhorse,
so heavier stallions were used to increase its
size. From then, Spanish stock was also used.
• **CHARACTERISTICS** In the 17th century,
two types emerged: the small, fast *mareyeur*, for
delivering fish from Boulogne; and the heavy,
agricultural horse, which is
still bred.

INFLUENCES

SPANISH
Gave soundness
of leg, better
constitution, and
increased activity.

ARABIAN
Transmitted its
refinement and
spirit; greatly
improved action.

FOREST HORSE
Supplied the
basis for the
considerable size
and substance.

*refined, graceful
head is evidence of
oriental influence*

HEIGHT
Stands between 15.3 and 16.3hh.

FRANCE: BOULOGNE

*prominently
veined skin*

*muscular legs
have short, thick
cannons*

Colors Gray	Uses Heavy Draft

Environment Cool temperate	Origin Middle Ages	Blood Cold

BRETON

The Breton is the indigenous horse of north-west France. It is based on the primitive horse of the Black Mountains. At one time, there were four distinct types, one of which was a riding horse. Two types are now recognized: the massive draft and the lighter Breton Postier.

• **BREEDING** The heavy draft Breton was developed from crosses to the Ardennais, Boulonnais, and Percheron. The smaller Postier carries Boulonnais and Percheron blood and also some Norfolk Roadster. Both types share one studbook. They are selectively bred and performance tested in harness.

• **CHARACTERISTICS** The heavy draft, an early maturing horse, is in demand for meat. The Postier, a clean-legged horse, like a lightweight Suffolk Punch, displays energy and freedom at the trot. Once used as an artillery horse, it is ideal for light agricultural draft and is used to improve less developed stock.

FRANCE: BLACK MOUNTAINS

tail is customarily docked, like that of • *the Norman Cob*

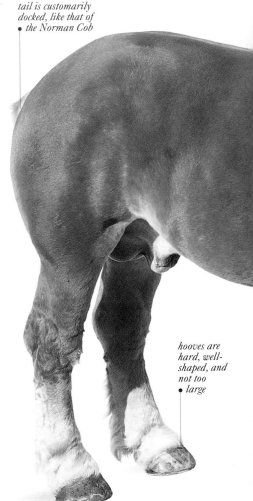

hooves are hard, well-shaped, and not too • *large*

INFLUENCES

BOULONNAIS Transmitted refinement and greater freedom of action.

ARDENNAIS Was used to increase the size, substance, and weight.

PERCHERON Complemented the Boulonnais' qualities, giving great strength.

NORFOLK ROADSTER Gave robust constitution and trotting ability.

Colors Roan, Chestnut	Uses Heavy Draft, Light Draft

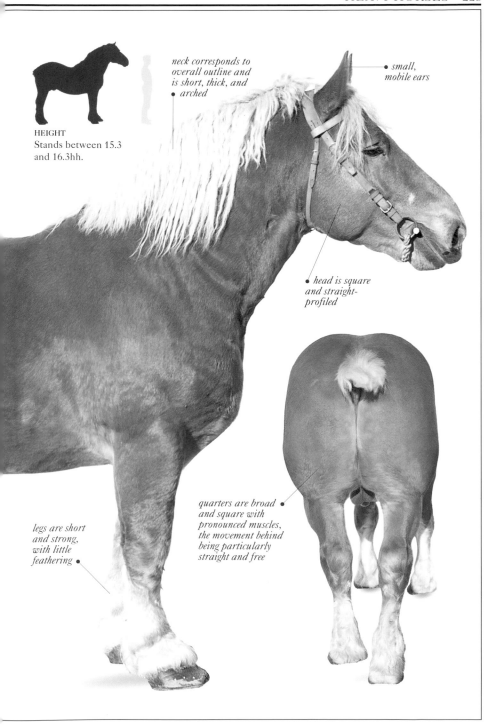

neck corresponds to overall outline and is short, thick, and arched •

• small, mobile ears

HEIGHT
Stands between 15.3 and 16.3hh.

• head is square and straight-profiled

quarters are broad • and square with pronounced muscles, the movement behind being particularly straight and free

legs are short and strong, with little feathering •

Environment Cool temperate	Origin 18th century	Blood Cold

PERCHERON

The attractive Percheron, an elegant horse owing much to
Arabian blood, is one of the most popular heavy breeds. One
authority described it as "an Arabian influenced by the
climate and the agricultural work for which it has been used
for centuries." The Percheron, much appreciated because of
its lack of feathering, a frequent cause of skin problems,
was exported extensively to Canada and the USA.

FRANCE: NORMANDY

• **BREEDING** The Percheron originated in the limestone
region of La Perche, Normandy. Its ancestors may have
carried the knights of Charles Martel, who broke the Muslim
invasion of Europe at Tours in AD 732. It is claimed that, from
then, oriental blood was available to French breeders. More
Eastern blood was used after the 11th century, and
Arabian sires were used at Le Pin from 1760. The
most influential Percheron lines are dominated
by Arabian crosses, particularly that of the
stallion Jean le Blanc, foaled in 1830. Despite
this, the breed has lost none of its size and
power. The world's biggest horse was the
Percheron Dr. Le Gear. He stood at 21hh and
weighed 3,024 lb (1,372 kg).

• **CHARACTERISTICS** The Percheron has
filled many roles: warhorse, coach horse, farmhorse, and has even been used under saddle. The
breed is hardy, versatile, and very even-tempered.
Like the Boulonnais, the action is long, low, and
free, and distinguishes it from other heavy breeds.

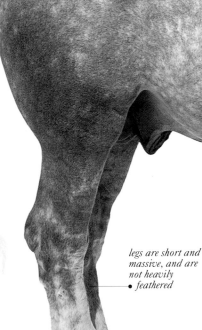

*legs are short and
massive, and are
not heavily
• feathered*

*fine head has long •
ears, large eyes, and
a broad forehead*

Colors Gray, Black	Uses Heavy Draft

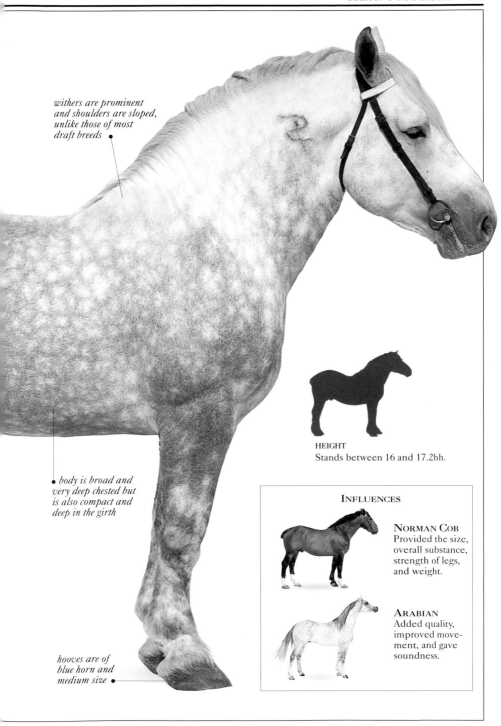

withers are prominent and shoulders are sloped, unlike those of most draft breeds

body is broad and very deep chested but is also compact and deep in the girth

hooves are of blue horn and medium size

HEIGHT
Stands between 16 and 17.2hh.

INFLUENCES

NORMAN COB
Provided the size, overall substance, strength of legs, and weight.

ARABIAN
Added quality, improved move-ment, and gave soundness.

Environment Cool temperate	Origin 19th–20th century	Blood Cold

NORMAN COB

The enduring, ever popular Norman Cob is still produced at the centuries-old studs of Le Pin and Sainte Lô in Normandy. It is less well known than the prestigious French Trotters, Percherons, Thoroughbreds, Boulonnais, and Anglo-Normans resident at both centers.

• **BREEDING** At the end of the 19th century, a distinction was made between cavalry remounts and heavier, light-draft type horses. The tails of the light-draft type were docked according to the custom and the horses were called cobs, after their British counterparts. These horses were documented and performance tested, but were never entered in a studbook, although many stallions were kept at both studs.

• **CHARACTERISTICS** Norman Cobs are still used for agricultural work, especially in the La Manche region, with which they are closely associated. They are heavier than previously, but retain their energetic pace at the trot.

FRANCE: LA MANCHE, NORMANDY

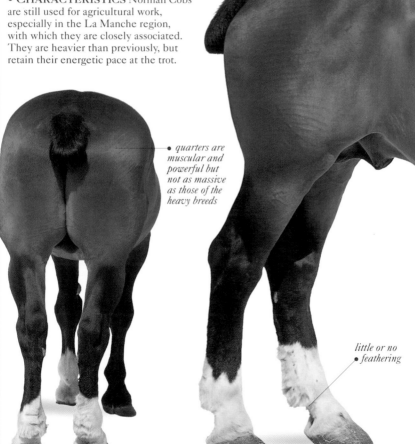

quarters are muscular and powerful but not as massive as those of the heavy breeds

little or no feathering

Colors Chestnut, Bay	Uses Light Draft

strong, crested neck
and sensible head are
characteristic ●

● back is short

good shoulders allow
great freedom at trot –
● the working pace

● body is compact
and stocky, like that
of the English Cob

legs are short and
have good bone
measurement ●

HEIGHT
Stands between 15.3 and 16.3hh.

INFLUENCE

NORMAN DRAFT
Provided base of
size, strength,
and weight.

Environment Cool temperate	Origin 18th century	Blood Cold

CLYDESDALE

The Clydesdale Horse Society was formed in Britain in 1877 and in the following year the American Clydesdale Society was founded. Within a short time, the breed was firmly established in both the USA and Canada, and overseas sales became a notable feature in Clydesdale breeding. Clydesdales were also exported in considerable numbers to Germany, Russia, Japan, South Africa, Australia, and New Zealand.

UK: LANARKSHIRE, SCOTLAND

• **BREEDING** The breed originated in Clyde Valley, Scotland. In the 18th century, the Duke of Hamilton and John Paterson of Lochlyoch imported Flemish stallions. The object was to increase the size of the small native draft horse. Shire blood was also used to such an extent that it could be claimed that Shire and Clydesdale were two branches of a single breed. Nonetheless, by the 19th century, breeders had produced an entirely distinctive breed of draft horse.

• **CHARACTERISTICS** Of lighter build than the Shire, the Clydesdale is noted for its very active paces. Although bred for agricultural work, this versatile breed is particularly suited to heavy urban draft.

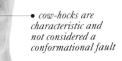

• *cow-hocks are characteristic and not considered a conformational fault*

• *head is finer than most draft breeds, with a straight, rather than convex, profile*

feathering is heavy, but not coarse •

Colors Bay, Roan with White	Uses Heavy Draft

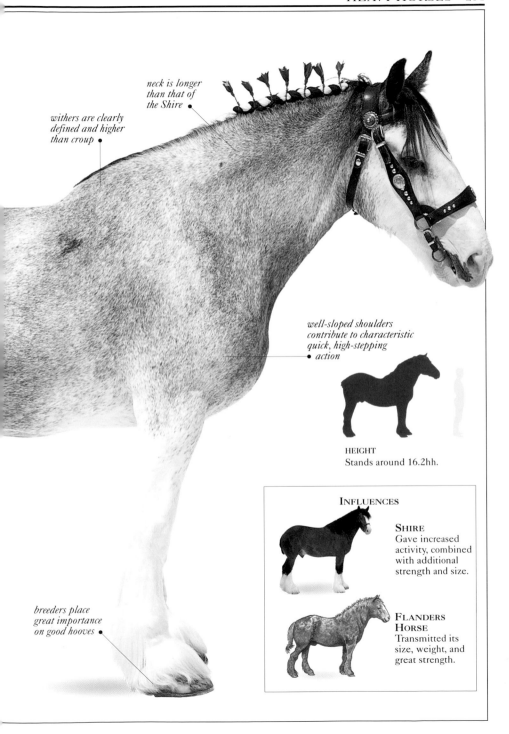

*neck is longer
than that of
the Shire •*

*withers are clearly
defined and higher
than croup •*

*well-sloped shoulders
contribute to characteristic
quick, high-stepping
• action*

HEIGHT
Stands around 16.2hh.

*breeders place
great importance
on good hooves •*

INFLUENCES

SHIRE
Gave increased
activity, combined
with additional
strength and size.

**FLANDERS
HORSE**
Transmitted its
size, weight, and
great strength.

Environment Cool temperate	Origin 18th century	Blood Cold

SUFFOLK PUNCH

The Suffolk Punch is entirely distinctive due to its "chesnut" coloring (the Suffolk Horse Society always employs that peculiar spelling) and its general appearance. "Punch" is often defined as a short-legged, barrel-bodied English horse – "a short, fat fellow," an apt description of this breed. This East Anglian horse is the oldest and purest of the British heavy breeds. All Suffolks trace their descent from one stallion, Thomas Crisp's Horse of Ufford (Orford), foaled in 1768.

UK: SUFFOLK, ENGLAND

• **BREEDING** It is very likely that the early Suffolks were influenced by the Norfolk Roadsters, developed in East Anglia from the 16th century on. It is also probable that the active-trotting Flanders mares, which were also mainly chestnut, played a part in the breed's evolution.

• **CHARACTERISTICS** The Suffolk is an all-around farmhorse. Its legs have no feathering, making it suitable for work on heavy clay lands. It is also an immensely powerful draft horse that was once in great demand in the cities and towns. The breed is long-lived, early maturing, and economical to keep – as it needs less feed than other horses of similar size and type. The action at the trot is especially energetic.

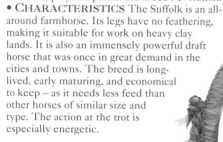

• *quarters are massive and rounded and complement the breed's endearing "roly-poly" character*

• *hooves are small for a draft horse, but are hard and sound*

• *relatively large head has a broad forehead and a straight or slightly convex profile*

Colors Chestnut	Uses Heavy Draft

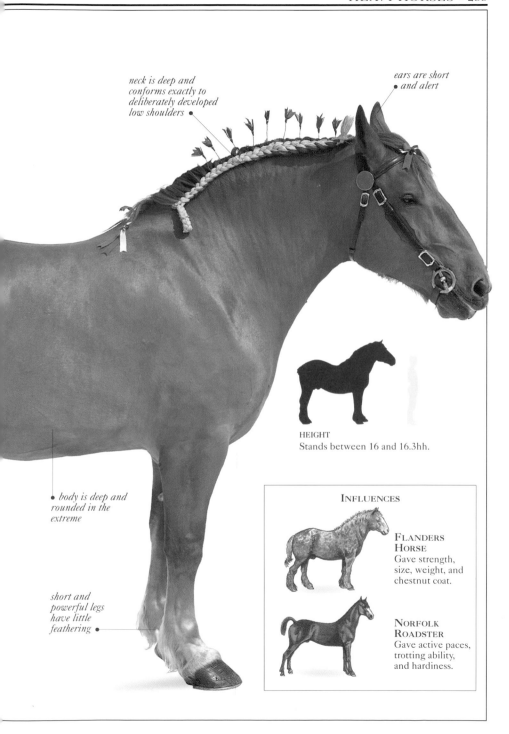

neck is deep and conforms exactly to deliberately developed low shoulders

ears are short and alert

body is deep and rounded in the extreme

short and powerful legs have little feathering

HEIGHT
Stands between 16 and 16.3hh.

INFLUENCES

FLANDERS HORSE
Gave strength, size, weight, and chestnut coat.

NORFOLK ROADSTER
Gave active paces, trotting ability, and hardiness.

Environment Cool temperate	Origin 19th century	Blood Cold

SHIRE

The Shire is considered the supreme draft horse. It is remarkably popular in Britain and, if anything, its numbers are on the increase. The name Shire derives from the English shires of Lincoln, Leicester, Stafford, and Derby.

• **BREEDING** The breed descends from England's Great Horse of the Middle Ages, which was subsequently known as the English, or Old English, Black. During the 16th and 17th centuries, the native stock was much influenced by Flanders horses. These had been imported by Dutch contractors who were draining the English fenlands. The active black Friesian was another element. The Shire's foundation stallion was the Packington Blind Horse. He stood at Ashby-de-la-Zouche between 1755 and 1770 and appears in the first studbook, published in 1878. In 1884, the Shire Horse Society replaced the English Cart Horse Society and the name "Shire" came into being.

• **CHARACTERISTICS** The Shire is noted for its great strength and is probably the heaviest of the draft breeds. Its weight, when full grown, may be 2,240–2,688 lb (1,016–1,219 kg). Despite its size and strength, it is essentially gentle and is easily managed.

UK: MIDLANDS, ENGLAND

bone measurement is 11–12 in (28–30 cm)

HEIGHT
Stands between 16.2 and 17.2hh.

INFLUENCES

FRIESIAN
Improved the breed's carriage, and added to its freedom of action.

FLANDERS HORSE
Provided the great strength, size, and weight.

Colors Black, Bay, Gray	Uses Heavy Draft

relatively
long neck •

overall structure is one of
strength, with width across
the body and short,
• thick musculature

shoulders are
wide and deep to
• accommodate a collar

the girth of a full •
grown Shire may be
6–8 ft (1.8–2.4 m)

lower legs are heavily
feathered with fine,
silky hair •

• head is broad between
large and kindly eyes, and
nose is Roman (convex)

Environment Temperate, Controlled	Origin 18th–19th century	Blood Cold

ITALIAN HEAVY DRAFT

The Italian Heavy Draft, often termed the Italian Agricultural Horse, was once the most popular heavy horse in Italy. It was bred extensively in northern and central Italy, particularly around Venice. Today, the horse is used for meat as well as for work, and its numbers are decreasing.

• **BREEDING** Before the establishment of a national heavy draft breed, Italy relied on imports of Brabant horses from Belgium. These animals were crossed with local mares. As the results were not entirely suitable, further crosses were made with the Boulonnais and Percheron. Finally, this much improved stock was crossed with the clean-legged, fast-trotting Breton Postier, itself influenced by the Norfolk Trotter. The resultant stock was quick-moving and of smaller proportions, and was ideal for light draft and farm work. The relatively swift trotting action gave rise to the Italian breed title, *Tiro Pesante Rapido*.

• **CHARACTERISTICS** The overall conformation reflects the strong influence of the Breton. There is also a suggestion of the lighter Avelignese, which may have been involved in the base stock. The Italian Heavy Draft is generally a compact, symmetrical animal with a surprisingly fine head. Some coarseness is apparent in the legs, round joints, and boxy hooves. It is kind and willing, and it has an energetic action.

ITALY: NORTHERN AND CENTRAL

hooves are often small and boxy, reflecting the weakness of base stock

HEIGHT
Stands between 15 and 16hh.

INFLUENCE

BRETON
Active movement was derived from this fast-trotting breed.

Colors Chestnut, Roan	Uses Draft

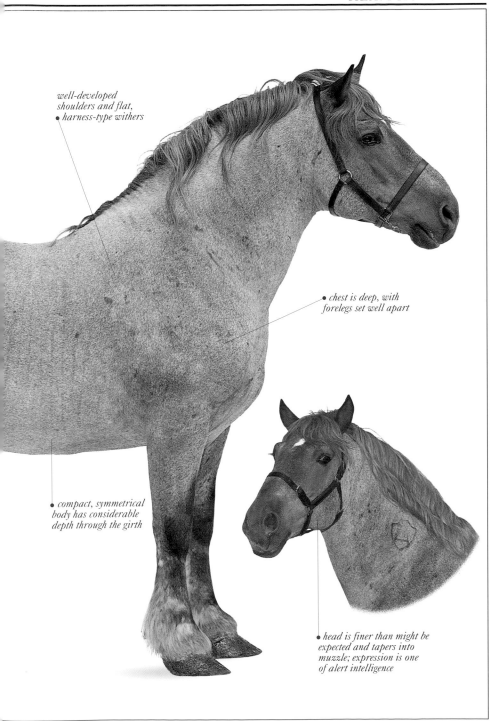

well-developed
shoulders and flat,
• harness-type withers

• chest is deep, with
forelegs set well apart

• compact, symmetrical
body has considerable
depth through the girth

• head is finer than might be
expected and tapers into
muzzle; expression is one
of alert intelligence

TYPES

Environment Temperate, Controlled	Origin 18th–19th century	Blood Warm

HUNTER

The hunter is a type indigenous to Britain and Ireland. It is not a breed, because it lacks fixed common characteristics and varies according to the requirements of the country in which it is ridden. In strongly fenced, grass country, for instance, a near-Thoroughbred horse is required. In countries where speed is not of the essence, a sensible halfbreed horse, with staying power and the ability to jump, is more suitable.

• **BREEDING** The best hunters are those bred in Britain and Ireland, where hunting has been a part of rural life for centuries. Often, both Irish and English hunters are based on a cross between the Irish Draft and the Thoroughbred. Many good horses also carry pony blood, some may be Cleveland Bay crosses, and others have draft horse blood in their ancestry. Whatever the mix, the best hunters always have a good proportion of Thoroughbred blood to give speed, courage, and athletic ability.

• **CHARACTERISTICS** A hunter must be sound, well-proportioned, and have all the conformational attributes of a good riding horse. He needs to be well-balanced, quick, and sufficiently bold to tackle every sort of obstacle in all riding conditions. He should be temperate, have good manners, and a robust constitution.

UK AND IRELAND

• *legs built for strength and speed*

hooves must be exemplary •

INFLUENCES

THOROUGHBRED Provided the essential scope and boldness in the hunter.

IRISH DRAFT Supplied bone, substance, and a sensible outlook.

CLEVELAND BAY Imparted bone, size, and the jumping ability.

Colors All, including part	Uses Saddle

HEIGHT
Stands between
15.2 and 17hh.

• *this hunter has a great
"front" beyond the saddle
and corresponding length
over the neck's topline*

• *compact body
with well-sprung
ribs and ample
depth through girth*

• *the best hunters
show quality in
their heads, with an
honest, workman-
like outlook*

Environment Temperate, Controlled	Origin 18th–19th century	Blood Warm, Hot

HACK

The modern hack, a British phenomenon, is essentially a show horse of supreme elegance, full of presence, beautifully balanced in its paces, and with perfect manners.

• **BREEDING** The majority of show hacks are Thoroughbred, although some may be Anglo-Arabs or halfbreeds. In the past, a distinction was made between the "covert" hack, which conveyed the rider to the hunt meet, and the more refined "park" hack, which fashionable socialites rode in places like London's Rotten Row. Modern show hacks are the equivalent of the latter, while "riding horses" take the place of the covert hacks and have their own classes.

• **CHARACTERISTICS** A hack has to be a model of good conformation. Although light and graceful, it must be neither ponyish, nor gangly, and it is expected to have 8 in (20 cm) of bone below the knee.

INFLUENCES

THOROUGHBRED Gave elegance, balance, good conformation, and movement.

ANGLO-ARAB Provided similar elegance with a more equable temperament.

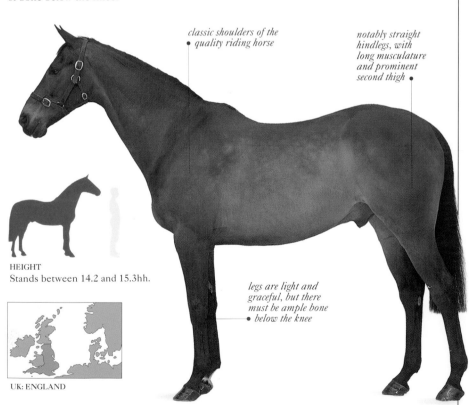

classic shoulders of the • quality riding horse

notably straight hindlegs, with long musculature and prominent second thigh •

HEIGHT
Stands between 14.2 and 15.3hh.

legs are light and graceful, but there must be ample bone • below the knee

UK: ENGLAND

Colors All solid	Uses Saddle

Environment Temperate, Controlled	Origin 20th century	Blood Warm

RIDING PONY

The riding pony is the juvenile's equivalent of the show hack, but, while having the proportions of the Thoroughbred, it retains the essential pony look and character. In Britain, show ring riding ponies are exhibited in three divisions: up to 12.2hh, up to 13.2hh, and up to 14.2hh.

• **BREEDING** The riding pony has evolved in Britain over the last half-century as a result of a skillful amalgam of bloods. It represents a remarkable accomplishment in the history of horse breeding. The base stock was largely Welsh ponies (Sections A and B), or ponies with Welsh and possibly some Arabian blood. These were crossed with small Thoroughbred sires of polo type, and at least one notable strain descends from an Arabian, the stallion Naseel.

• **CHARACTERISTICS** The action is free, long, and similar to the Thoroughbred. Ideally, it retains some of the substance of its native forebear and a lot of its good sense.

INFLUENCES

THOROUGHBRED
Gave long, low action; provided extra brilliance and quality.

WELSH A
Gave essential pony character and added to the substance.

ARABIAN
Added to soundness of leg and manageable temperament.

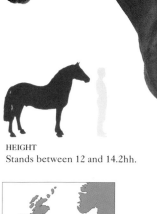

HEIGHT
Stands between 12 and 14.2hh.

UK: ENGLAND

overall outline and •
proportion is a scaled-down version of the hack

Colors All solid	Uses Saddle

| Environment Temperate, Controlled | Origin 18th–19th century | Blood Warm |

COB

The cob is one of the most appealing horses. Although it is immediately recognizable, it is not a breed, for there is no set pattern to its production. In Britain, the cob is still an all-around horse and will often, in the old Roadster tradition, go as well in harness as under saddle.

• **BREEDING** Some very good cobs are bred in Ireland from Irish Draft crosses, and some are pure Irish Draft. Welsh Cobs are another source, and there are cobs that have been bred from heavy horse breeds crossed with small Thoroughbreds, or from Cleveland Bays. On the whole, the breeding of cobs is likely to be accidental rather than deliberate.

• **CHARACTERISTICS** Cobs (those standing up to 15.1hh) are exhibited in British show classes with their manes roached, and are expected to walk, trot, canter, and gallop. The traditional practice of roaching sets off the strong, short neck and gives the horse a jaunty, sporting look. Otherwise, the cob is thickset, with powerful quarters and short, strong legs. It is a structure that is predisposed to the carrying of weight rather than to speed, although cobs are still expected to gallop and jump. Above all, a cob, while being a "character," must also have the best of manners. He is considered to be a "gentleman's gentleman," and is expected to behave as such.

IRELAND, AND UK: ENGLAND

• *legs have plenty of bone*

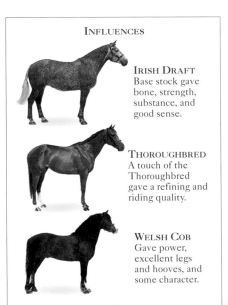

INFLUENCES

IRISH DRAFT
Base stock gave bone, strength, substance, and good sense.

THOROUGHBRED
A touch of the Thoroughbred gave a refining and riding quality.

WELSH COB
Gave power, excellent legs and hooves, and some character.

| Colors All, including part | Uses Saddle, Harness |

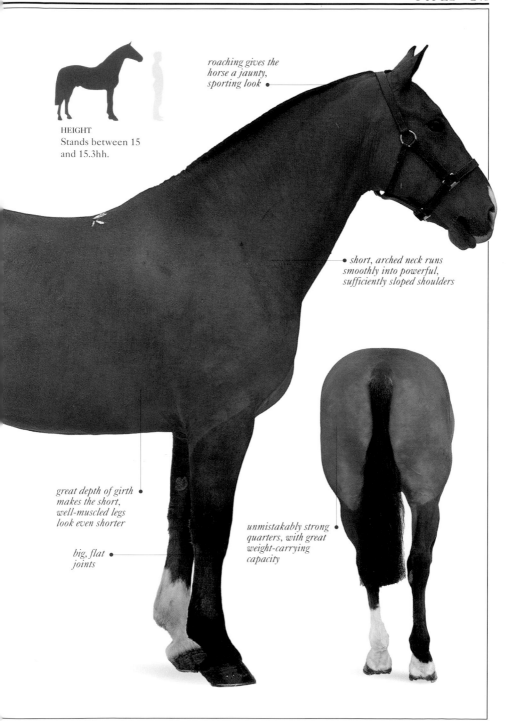

roaching gives the
horse a jaunty,
sporting look •

HEIGHT
Stands between 15
and 15.3hh.

• short, arched neck runs
smoothly into powerful,
sufficiently sloped shoulders

great depth of girth •
makes the short,
well-muscled legs
look even shorter

big, flat •
joints

unmistakably strong •
quarters, with great
weight-carrying
capacity

Environment Temperate, Controlled	Origin 19th–20th century	Blood Warm, Hot

POLO PONY

Although the polo pony is not a breed (nor a pony any more), it is a specifically developed type and is recognizable by its outline and general appearance. Originally, height limits were imposed under the rules of the game of polo, but these were abolished after World War 1 and now the height of the average polo pony is about 15.1hh.

• **BREEDING** The ancient game of polo originated in Persia as long ago as 525 BC, and was introduced to Europe and the Americas by the British, who had learned the game in India. British-bred ponies were based on native pony mares crossed with small Thoroughbreds, but today's pony is likely to have strong Argentine connections. The Argentinians dominate the game and have the facilities to produce quality ponies in quantity. They imported Thoroughbreds and crossed them with the tough, halfbreed Criollo stock, putting the progeny back to the Thoroughbred to increase speed. In recent years, American Quarter Horses have also become an element in polo pony breeding.

• **CHARACTERISTICS** The polo pony is distinctly Thoroughbred in appearance. It has to be fast, courageous, balanced, and very agile. A long, low stride is not a necessary attribute, as it is easier to hit the ball from a shorter-striding pony.

ARGENTINA

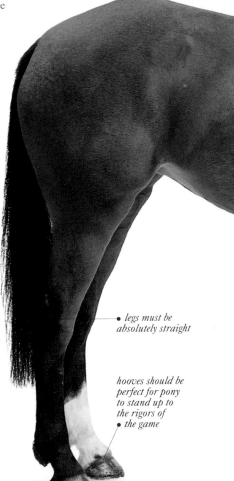

• *legs must be absolutely straight*

hooves should be perfect for pony to stand up to the rigors of • *the game*

head is wiry and • *clean, without fleshiness*

Colors All, including part	Uses Saddle

HEIGHT
Stands around 15.1hh.

mane is always roached, to avoid interference with the stick •

• *typically lean, graceful neck and very prominent withers*

short cannons and good bone are characteristic •

INFLUENCES

THOROUGHBRED
Imparted its speed, quick responses, agility, and courage.

QUARTER HORSE
Gave speed, intelligence, agility, and responsiveness.

CRIOLLO
The wiry base stock was tough, sound, hardy, and sagacious.

HORSE CREDITS

We are indebted to the many owners and breeders who allowed their horses to be photographed for this book; without their cooperation, it could not have been produced. The horses are listed in page order, accompanied by the name of the breed, the name of the horse, and the name and brief address of the owner.

PONIES

• 48 *Icelandic Horse*: Leiknir, Kentucky Horse Park, USA
• 50 *Fjord Pony*: Maple Klaus, John Goddard Fenwick and Lyn Moran, Ausdan Stud, UK
• 52 *Gotland*: Ripadals Benni 398, Carina Andersson, Sweden
• 54 *Huçul*: Lubas, Janusz Utrata, Poland
• 56 *Konik*: Hewal, S J Skoki, Poland
• 58 *Haflinger*: Nomad, Miss Helen Blair, Silvretta Haflinger Stud, UK
• 60 *Ariègeois*: Radium, Haras National de Tarbes, France
• 62 *Landais*: Hippolyte, Haras National de Pau, France
• 63 *Pottock*: Thouarec III, Haras National de Pau, France
• 64 *Shetland*: Chatsworth Belle, Mrs Hampton, Briar Stud, UK
• 66 *Highland*: Nashend Sabine, Mr and Mrs Clive Smith, Nashend Stud, UK
• 68 *Dales*: Warrenlane Duke, Mr Dickinson, Millbeck Pony Stud, UK
• 69 *Fell*: Waverhead William, Mr and Mrs Errington, UK
• 70 *Hackney Pony*: Hurstwood Consort, Mr and Mrs Hayden, Hurstwood Stud, UK
• 72 *Exmoor*: Murrayton Delphinus, June Freeman, Murrayton Stud, UK
• 73 *Dartmoor*: Allendale Vampire, Miss M Houlden, Haven Stud, UK
• 74 *New Forest Pony*: Bowerwood Aquila, Mrs Ray Turner, Bowerwood Stud, UK
• 76 *Connemara*: Garryhack Tooreen, Mrs Beckett, Shipton Connemara Pony Stud, UK
• 78 *Welsh Mountain Pony*: Bengad Dark Mullein, Mrs C Bowyer, Symondsbury Stud, UK
• 79 *Welsh Pony*: Twyford Signal, Mr and Mrs L E Bigley, Llanarth Stud, UK
• 80 *Welsh Pony of Cob Type*: Llygedyn Solo, Kitty Williams, Glebedale Stud, UK
• 82 *Bardigiano*: Pippo, Istituto Incremento Ippico di Crema, Italy
• 84 *Sorraia*: Giro, Portuguese National Stud (EFPAA), Portugal
• 86 *Skyrian Horse*: Mitsibonas, Dinos Maroudis, Greece
• 87 *Pindos Pony*: Maro, Penny Turner, Greece
• 88 *Caspian*: Hopstone Shabdiz, Mrs Scott, Henden Caspian Stud, UK
• 90 *Bashkir*: Mel's Lucky Boy, Dan Stewart Family, Kentucky Horse Park, USA
• 92 *Australian Pony*: Australian Pony Promotion Group, Pitchwood Stud, Australia
• 94 *American Shetland*: Little Trouble, Marvin McCabe, Kentucky Horse Park, USA
• 96 *Rocky Mountain Pony*: Mocha Monday, Rea Swan, Kentucky Horse Park, USA
• 98 *Chincoteague*: Clover, Kenneth Burton, USA
• 99 *Sable Island Pony*: (State of) Nova Scotia, Canada
• 100 *Galiceno*: Java Gold, Billy Jack Jiles, Texas, USA
• 102 *Falabella*: Pegasus of Kilverstone, Lady Fisher, Kilverstone Wildlife Park, UK

HORSES

• 104 *Døle Gudbrandsdal*: Pajagutt, Gunnar Skjervheim, Norway
• 106 *Finnish Horse*: Oikka, Hevostalouden Tutkimusasema, Finland
• 108 *Swedish Warmblood*: Asterix 694, Swedish National Stud, Sweden
• 110 *Frederiksborg*: Zarif Langløkkegard, Harry Nielsen, Denmark
• 112 *Knabstruper*: Føniks, Poul Elmerkjær, Denmark
• 114 *Danish Warmblood*: Rambo, Jorgen Olsen, Denmark
• 116 *Friesian*: Sjouke, Sonia Gray, Tattondale Carriages, UK
• 118 *Gelderlander*: Spooks, Peter Munt, Ascot Driving Stables, UK
• 120 *Groningen*: Elza, Mr J Dank, Netherlands
• 122 *Dutch Warmblood*: Edison, Mrs Dejonge, UK
• 124 *Belgian Warmblood*: Didi, Mr A Schwartz, Belgium
• 126 *Trakehner*: Nemo, Ileen Poole, Canada
• 128 *Wielkopolski*: Snapjack, Mrs S Bates, UK
• 130 *Bavarian Warmblood*: Donator, Mr John Hindle, UK
• 131 *Hanoverian*: Défilante, Barry Mawdsley, European Horse Enterprises, UK
• 132 *Holsteiner*: Lenard, Sue Watson, Trenawin Stud, UK
• 134 *Oldenburg*: Renoir, Louise Tomkins, UK
• 136 *Württemberg*: Tees Hanaeur, Mrs Tees, UK
• 138 *Rhinelander*: Arabella, Mrs Lucinda Marchessini, UK
• 140 *Nonius*: Pampas & 141 *Furioso*: Furioso IV: both owned by A G Kishumseigi, Hungary
• 142 *Shagya Arab*: Artaxerxes, Jeanette Bauch and Jens Brinksten, Denmark
• 144 *Lipizzaner*: Siglavy Szella, J G Fenwick and L Moran, Ausdan Stud, UK

- **146** *Selle Français*: Prince D'elle, Haras National de Saint Lô, France
- **147** *French Trotter*: Pur Historien, Haras National de Compiègne, France
- **148** *Camargue*: Redounet, Mr Contreras, France
- **150** *Anglo-Arab*: Restif, Haras National de Compiègne, France
- **152** *Thoroughbred*: Amoco Park, Spruce Meadows, Canada
- **154** *Hackney Horse*: Whiteavon Step High, David Vyse, UK
- **156** *Cleveland Bay*: Oaten Mainbrace, Mr and Mrs Dimock, UK
- **157** *Irish Draft*: Miss Mill, Mr R J Lampard, UK
- **158** *Welsh Cob*: Treflys Jacko, Mr and Mrs L E Bigley, Llanarth Stud, UK
- **160** *Salerno*: Jeraz, Sig. Giorgio Caponitti, Italy
- **162** *Sardinian*: O'Hara, Sig. P Adriano, Italy
- **164** *Maremmana*: Barone, Mr Attilio Tavazzani, Centro Ippico De Castelverde, Italy
- **165** *Murgese*: Obscuro, Istituto Incremento Ippico di Crema, Italy
- **166** *Andalusian*: Campanero XXIV, Nigel Oliver, Singleborough Stud, UK
- **168** *Lusitano*: Montemere-O-Nova (Romano), Nan Thurman, Turville Valley Stud, UK
- **170** *Alter-Real*: Castro, Portuguese National Stud (EFPAA), Portugal
- **172** *Barb*: Taw's Little Buck, Kentucky Horse Park, USA
- **174** *Arabian*: Altruista, Pat and Joanna Maxwell, Lodge Farm Arabian Stud, UK
- **176** *Akhal-Teke*: Fafakir-Bola, Moscow Agricultural Academy, Russia
- **178** *Budenny*: Barin, Moscow Agricultural Academy, Russia
- **180** *Kabardin*: Daufuz, Korache Stud, Russia
- **181** *Karabakh*: Moscow Race Track, Russia
- **182** *Orlov Trotter*: Moscow Hippodrome, Russia
- **184** *Don*: Bageg, Moscow Agricultural Academy, Russia
- **186** *Przewalski's Horse*: Marwell Zoological Park, UK
- **188** *Kathiawari*: refer to publisher
- **190** *Indianbred*: refer to publisher
- **192** *Australian Stock Horse*: Scrumlo Victory, Mrs R Waller, Ophir Stud, Australia
- **194** *Saddlebred*: Dr Technical, Adrian Neufeld, Canada
- **196** *Appaloosa*: Golden Nugget, Sally Chaplin, UK
- **198** *Missouri Fox Trotter*: Easy Street, Ruth Massey, Kentucky Horse Park, USA
- **200** *Morgan*: Fox Creek's Dynasty, Darwin Olsen, Kentucky Horse `Park, USA
- **202** *Mustang*: Patrick, Kentucky Horse Park, USA
- **203** *Palomino*: Golden Wildfire, Monica Comm, Canada
- **204** *Pinto*: Hit Man, Boyd Cantrell, Kentucky Horse Park, USA
- **206** *Quarter Horse*: Mr Starpasser (Dexter), Pat Buckler, Canada
- **208** *Tennessee Walking Horse*: Midnight Toddy, Grethe Broholm, Canada
- **209** *Standardbred*: Rambling Willie, Farrington Stables and the Estate of Paul Siebert, Kentucky Horse Park, USA
- **210** *Colorado Ranger*: Skippers Valentine, T J Crouch, Texas, USA
- **212** *Criollo*: Azulecha, Clare Tomlinson, UK
- **213** *Paso*: Medianoche, D McIntosh, Canada

HEAVY HORSES
- **214** *North Swedish Horse*: Ysterman, Ingvar Andersson, Sweden
- **216** *Jutland*: Tempo, Jørgen Neilsen, Denmark
- **218** *Brabant*: Roy, Kentucky Horse Park, USA
- **220** *Noriker*: Dinolino, Mr J Waldhem, Germany
- **222** *Ardennais*: Ramses du Vallon, Haras National de Pau, France
- **223** *Boulonnais*: Urus, Haras National de Compiègne, France
- **224** *Breton*: Ulysses, Haras National de Tarbes, France
- **226** *Percheron*: Tango & **228** *Norman Cob*: Ibis: owned by Haras National de Saint Lô, France
- **230** *Clydesdale*: Blue Print, Mervyn and Pauline Ramage, Mount Farm Clydesdale Horses, UK
- **232** *Suffolk Punch*: Laurel Keepsake II, P Adams and Sons, UK
- **234** *Shire*: Duke, Jim Lockwood, Courage Shire Horse Centre, UK
- **236** *Italian Heavy Draft*: Nobile, Istituto Incremento Ippico di Crema, Italy

TYPES
- **238** *Hunter:* Hobo; **240** *Hack*: Rye Tangle; **241** *Riding Pony*: Brutt; **242** *Cob*: Super Ted: all owned by Robert Oliver, UK
- **244** *Polo Pony*: refer to publisher

GLOSSARY

ALTHOUGH TECHNICAL EXPRESSIONS have been avoided wherever possible, a limited use of them is unavoidable in a book of this nature. Many of the terms listed below are unique to horses and the equestrian world. Words that appear in bold type are explained elsewhere in the glossary, and you may also find it helpful to look at the annotated illustrations on pp.18–19 in order to clarify some of the terms relating to horse anatomy.

• **ABOVE THE BIT**
When the horse carries its mouth above the level of the rider's hand, reducing the rider's control.

• **ABOVE THE GROUND**
Haute Ecole movements performed with either the forelegs or all four feet off the ground.

• **ACTION**
Movement of the skeletal frame in respect of locomotion.

• **AIRS**
Movements associated with classical or advanced equitation. (e.g. airs **above the ground**).

• **AGED**
Horse fifteen or more years old.

• **AGEING**
Process of estimating a horse's age by the appearance of the teeth.

• **AIDS**
Signals made by the rider or driver to communicate his wishes to the horse. "Natural" riding aids are the legs, hands, body weight, and voice. "Artificial" aids are the whip and spur.

• **AMBLE**
Slower form of the lateral pacing gait (see also **Pacer**).

• **ARTICULATION**
Where two or more bones meet to form a joint.

• **BACK AT THE KNEE**
Conformational fault in which forelegs are curved back below the knee. (Also called "Calf-knee" or "Buck-knee".)

• **BACK (TO BACK)**
First mounting of an unbroken horse (e.g. "this horse is ready to be backed").

• **BARREL**
Body between forearms and loins.

• **BARS (OF THE MOUTH)**
Area between the molars and incisors of the lower jaw on which the bit rests.

• **BLEMISH**
Permanent mark left by either an injury or disease.

• **BLOOD HORSE**
Thoroughbred horse.

• **BLOOD STOCK**
Thoroughbred horses bred to race.

• **BLOOD WEED**
Lightly built Thoroughbred horse that is of poor quality, lacking bone and substance.

• **BLUE FEET**
Dense, blue-black coloring of the horn.

• **BONE**
Measurement taken around the leg immediately below the knee or hock. Bone measurement determines ability to carry weight.

• **BOOK, THE**
See **General Studbook**.

• **BOSOMY**
Overwide and heavy chest.

• **BOTH LEGS FROM THE SAME HOLE**
Forelegs placed too close together because of an unduly narrow chest.

• **BOW-HOCKS**
Outward turned hock joints (opposite of **cow-hocks**).

• **BOXY HOOF**
Narrow, upright hoof with small **frog** and a closed heel. (Also called "club," "donkey," or "mule foot.")

• **BREAKING**
Early schooling or education of the horse for the various purposes for which it may be required.

• **BREED**
Equine group that has been bred selectively for consistent characteristics over an extended period. The pedigrees of a breed are entered in a **studbook**.

• **BROKEN COLORED**
Term applied to coats of two colors (e.g. skewbald, piebald). Generally refers to donkeys.

• **BROOD MARE**
Mare used for breeding.

• **BRUSHING**
Action of the hoof or shoe striking the opposite fetlock. Usually a conformational fault.

• **BUCK**
To leap in the air with the back arched, the horse coming down on stiff forelegs with lowered head.

• **BUNG TAIL**
Docked tail.

• **BY**
Used in conjunction with the sire, i.e. *by* so and so. (See also **Out of**.)

• **CANNON BONE**
Bone of foreleg between knee and fetlock. Also called "shin bone."

• **CARRIAGE HORSE**
Relatively light, elegant horse for private or hackney carriage use.

• **CART HORSE**
Heavy, **coldblood** draft horse.

• **CARTY**
Description of a horse of common appearance.

• **CAVALRY REMOUNT**
Horse used for service in an army unit. (Also called a "trooper.")

• **CAYUSE**
Tough American Indian pony descending from Spanish stock.

• **CHARGER**
Mount of military officers.

• **CHESTNUT (OR CASTOR)**
Small, horny excrescences on the inside of all four legs; or a coat color.

• **CHIN GROOVE**
Declivity above the lower lip in which the curb chain of the bit lies. (Also called "curb groove.")

• **CLEAN-LEGGED**
Without feather on the lower limbs.

• **CLOSE-COUPLED**
Short connections between component parts, with no slackness in the loins.

• **COACH HORSE**
Powerful, strongly built horse capable of drawing a heavy coach.

• **COARSE IN THE JOWL**
Notable fleshiness round the jowl, restricting the **flexion** of the head.

• **COFFIN HEAD**
Plain, ugly face with no prominence of the jowl.

- **COLDBLOOD**
Generic name for heavy, European horse breeds descended from the prehistoric Forest Horse.
- **COLT**
Uncastrated male horse under four years old. Male foals are denoted as "colt foals."
- **COMMON**
Horse of coarse appearance, usually the progeny of coldblood or nonpedigree parents.
- **COMMON BONE**
Bone of inferior quality; it is coarse-grained, lacking density, and with a large, central core.
- **COMMON-BRED**
Horse bred from mixed, non-pedigree parents.
- **CONFORMATION**
Manner in which the horse is "put together," with particular regard to its proportions.
- **COW-HOCKS**
Hocks that turn inward like those of a cow; the opposite to **bow-hocks**.
- **CROSSBRED**
Mating of unrelated horses; introduction of outside blood to the breed.
- **CROSSBREEDING**
Mating of purebred individuals of different breeds.
- **CROSSING OVER**
Faulty and dangerous **action** in which the feet cross over each other in movement.
- **CURB**
Thickening of the tendon or ligament below the point of the hock as a result of strain. "Curby hocks" are those affected by curbs, or those so shaped as to be predisposed to the formation of curbs.
- **DAISY-CUTTING**
Descriptive of low action at walk or trot, as characterized by Thorough-breds and Arabians.
- **DAM**
Horse's female parent.
- **DEEP GOING**
Wet or soft ground, made heavy by rain, into which the hooves sink.
- **DEPTH OF GIRTH**
Measurement from wither to elbow. "Good depth of girth" describes a generous measurement between the two points.
- **DIPPED BACK**
Descriptive of an unusually dipped back between withers and croup.

- **DISHED FACE**
Concave head profile, as exemplified by the Arabian.
- **DISHING**
Action of the foreleg when the toe is thrown outward in a circular movement. Considered faulty.
- **DOCK**
Part of the tail on which the hair grows; also the hairless underside.
- **DOCKING**
Amputation of the tail for the sake of appearance. Illegal in Britain.
- **DOUBLE MUSCLING**
Pronounced muscling at the croup found in some heavy horse breeds.
- **DROOPING QUARTERS**
Hindquarters with a pronounced fall away behind the croup.
- **ELK LIP**
Wide, overhanging upper lip.
- **ENTIRE**
Uncastrated male horse – a stallion.
- **ERGOT**
Horny growth on the back of the fetlock joint.
- **ESCUTCHEON**
Division of the hair below the point of the hips extending downward on the flanks.
- **EWE NECK**
Concavity of neck along its upper edge, with consequent protrusion of muscle on the underside.
- **EXTRAVAGANT ACTION**
High knee and hock action, as in Hackney and Saddlebred breeds.
- **FALSE RIBS**
Ten (asternal) ribs to the rear of the eight "true" (sternal) ribs.
- **FEATHER**
Long hair on the lower legs and fetlocks; abundant on heavy horses.
- **FILLY**
Female horse under four years old.
- **FIVE-GAITED**
Term for the Saddlebred horse, which is shown at the **slow gait** and **rack** as well as other paces
- **FLEXION**
A horse flexes when it yields the lower jaw to the bit, with the head bent at the poll. Also describes the full bending of the hock joints.
- **FOAL**
Colt, **gelding**, or **filly** up to the age of 12 months.
- **FOREHAND**
Horse's head, neck, shoulder, withers, and forelegs.
- **FORELOCK**
Extension of the mane lying between ears and over forehead.

- **FROG**
Rubbery, triangular pad of horn in the sole of the hoof, which acts as a shock absorber.
- **FULL MOUTH**
At six years, a horse with permanent teeth has a "full mouth."
- **GAITED HORSE**
American term for horse schooled to artificial as well as natural gaits.
- **GALVAYNE'S GROOVE**
Groove appearing on the corner incisor at ten years. It runs down the tooth reaching the bottom at about 20 years. Named after the l9th-century horse-tamer Sydney Galvayne.
- **GASKIN**
"Second thigh," extending from above the hock toward the stifle.
- **GELDING**
Castrated male horse.
- **GENERAL STUDBOOK**
Studbook in which are entered all Thoroughbred mares and their progeny foaled in the UK and the Republic of Ireland. Also known as "G.S.B." and "the Book."
- **GIRTH**
Circumference of the body measured from behind the withers around the barrel.
- **GOING**
Term indicating the nature of the ground, e.g. good, deep, rough.
- **GOOD FRONT**
Horse carrying its saddle behind a long, sloped shoulder and generous length of neck.
- **GOOSE-RUMP**
Pronounced muscular develop-ment at the croup, from whence the quarters run down to the tail. Also called the "jumper's bump".
- **GREASE**
Disease of the lower legs characterized by swelling, foul discharge, and irritation. Heavy horses with abundant feather are particularly vulnerable.
- **HACK**
Recognized type of light riding horse; or "to hack" – to go for a ride.
- **"HAIRIES"**
Originally a friendly name for heavy breeds, but now frequently applied to British mountain and moorland ponies.
- **HALTER-CLASS**
American term for classes of horses shown **in-hand**.

• **HAND**
Unit of measurement to describe horse's height (medieval origin). One hand equals 4 in (10 cm).

• **HARD HORSE**
Tough, enduring horse not susceptible to unsoundness or injury.

• **HARNESS**
Collective term for the equipment of a driven horse. Not applicable to the riding horse.

• **HARNESS HORSE**
Horse used in **harness**, having "harness"-type **conformation** (i.e. straighter shoulders, etc.), and, consequently, an elevated "harness action."

• *HAUTE ECOLE*
Classical art of advanced horsemanship.

• **HEAVY HORSE**
Any large draft horse.

• **HEAVY TOP**
Heavy body carried on disproportionately light legs.

• **HERRING-GUTTED**
Horse with a flat-sided, mean body running sharply upwards from **girth** to stifle.

• **HINDQUARTERS**
Body from the rear of the flank to the beginning of the tail, and down to the top of the **gaskin**.

• **HOCKS WELL LET DOWN**
Indicates short **cannon bones**, considered a structure of great strength. Long cannons are seen as a conformational weakness.

• **HOLLOW BACK**
See **Dipped Back**.

• **HOT**
If a horse becomes unduly excited is said to be "hot" or to "hot up."

• **HOTBLOOD**
Term describing Arabians, Barbs, and Thoroughbreds.

• **HYBRID**
Cross between a horse on one side and an ass, zebra, or other similar species on the other.

• **INBREEDING**
Mating of brother–sister, sire–daughter, son–**dam**, to fix or accentuate a particular characteristic.

• **IN FRONT OF THE BIT**
When a horse pulls or hangs heavily on the hands with its head outstretched.

• **IN-HAND**
Not ridden, as in show classes where horses are paraded around the arena in halters.

• **JIBBAH**
Peculiar bulged formation of the forehead of the Arabian horse.

• **JOG**
Short-paced trot.

• **LEAN HEAD**
Fine, very lightly skinned head, with muscles, veins, and bony protuberances showing clearly. Often described as a "dry" head in Arabians.

• **LIGHT HORSE**
Horse, other than a heavy horse or a pony, that is suitable for riding.

• **LIGHT OF BONE**
Insufficient bone below the knee to support weight of horse and rider without strain – and therefore a serious fault.

• **LINE BREEDING**
Mating of individuals with a common ancestor some generations removed, with the purpose of accentuating particular features.

• **LOADED SHOULDER**
Excessive muscle formation lying over and inhibiting the shoulder region.

• **LOINS**
Area either side of the spinal vertebrae lying immediately behind the saddle.

• **LOPE**
Slow Western canter performed with natural head carriage.

• **LOP EARS**
Ears that flop downward or are carried horizontally to either side. There is no effect upon performance or well-being.

• **MARE**
Female horse of four years old and upward.

• **MEALY NOSE**
Oatmeal-colored muzzle, as in the Exmoor pony.

• **MITBAH**
Angle at which the neck of the Arabian horse enters the head. This gives the arched set to the neck and enables near all-around movement of the neck.

• **NARROW BEHIND**
Deficiency in musculature of croup and thigh, giving a narrow appearance when viewed from behind.

• **NATIVE PONIES**
Another name for the British indigenous mountain and moorland breeds.

• **NICK**
Division and resetting of the muscles under the tail to give an artificially high carriage; or a mating likely to produce the desired offspring – "a good nick."

• **ON THE BIT**
A horse is said to be "on the bit" when he carries the head in a near-vertical plane, the mouth a little below the rider's hand.

• **ON THE LEG**
Describes a horse that is disproportionately long in the leg. It is a condition that is usually associated with inadequate depth in the body

• **ORIENTAL HORSE**
Term loosely applied to horses of Eastern origin, either Arabian or Barb, in use during the formative years of the English Thoroughbred.

• **OUT OF**
Used in conjunction with the **mare**, e.g. so-and-so *out of* so-and-so.

• **OVER AT THE KNEE**
Forward curve of the knees over the cannon, which may be the result of wear.

• **OVERBENT**
When the horse carries its mouth close to the chest to evade control. The horse is "behind the bit."

• **OVERSHOT MOUTH**
See **Parrot mouth**.

• **PACER**
Horse employing a lateral action at trot rather than the conventional diagonal movement, i.e. near fore and near hind together, followed by the offside pair.

• **PALFREY**
Medieval light saddle horse that could amble.

• **PARIETAL BONES**
Bones on the top of the skull.

• **PARROT MOUTH**
Malformation in which the incisors of the upper jaw overhang those of the lower jaw.

• **PEDIGREE**
Details of ancestry recorded in a **studbook**.

• **PENDULOUS LIP**
Flabby underlip hanging loose. Sometimes found in cart breeds and old **common-bred** horses.

• **PIGEON TOES**
Conformational fault in which the hooves are turned inward. (Also known as "pin-toes.")

• **PIG-EYE**
Small eye giving a mean and unintelligent expression.

- **POINTS**
External features of the horse, comprising its **conformation**; or a term relative to color, e.g. "bay with black points," meaning bay with black lower legs, mane, and tail.
- **PUREBRED**
Horse of any breed of pure pedigree blood.
- **QUALITY**
Element of refinement in breeds and types, usually due to Arabian or Thoroughbred influence.
- **QUARTERS**
See **Hindquarters**.
- **RACEHORSE**
Horse bred specifically for racing. This term usually refers to a Thoroughbred, but other breeds of horses are also raced.
- **RACK**
Fifth gait of the American Saddlebred – a fast, four-beat gait unrelated to pacing (see **Pacer**).
- **RAGGED HIPS**
Prominent hip bones lacking flesh and muscle.
- **RAM HEAD**
Convex profile like that of the Barb. Similar to **Roman nose**.
- **RANGY**
Description of a lanky horse having good scope of movement.
- **REMOUNT**
See **Cavalry remount**.
- **RHUM PONY**
Ancient strain of Highland pony.
- **RIBBED UP (WELL)**
Describes a short, deep body that is rounded, with well-sprung ribs.
- **RIDING HORSE**
Horse suitable for riding, having the **conformation** associated with comfortable riding **action** (as opposed to draft or carriage).
- **RISING**
Term used in ageing. A horse approaching five years is said to be "rising five."
- **ROACH BACK**
Convex curvature of the spine between wither and loin. Opposite to **dipped back**.
- **ROACHED MANE**
When the mane has been removed by clipping.
- **ROADSTER**
Trotting saddlehorse, ancestor of the modern Hackney, e.g. the Norfolk Roadster. In America, a light harness horse or pony, usually the Standardbred.

- **ROMAN NOSE**
Convex profile as found in the Shire and other heavy breeds.
- **SADDLE HORSE**
Riding horse; or a wooden trestle stand on which to put saddles.
- **SADDLE MARKS**
White hair in the saddle area probably caused by galls.
- **SCLERA**
White outer membrane of the eyeball. Characteristic of the Appaloosa.
- **SECOND THIGH**
See Gaskin.
- **SET TAIL**
Tail broken or **nicked** and set to give artificially high carriage.
- **SHANNON BONE**
Hind **cannon bone**.
- **SHORT-COUPLED**
See **Close-coupled**.
- **SHORT OF A RIB**
Conformational fault arising from **slack loins**, in which there is a marked space between the last rib and the hip. Occurs in overly long-backed horses.
- **SICKLE HOCKS**
Conformational fault in which, seen from the side, the hocks are angled too much at the joint, resulting in weak hindlegs.
- **SLAB-SIDED**
Horse with flat ribs.
- **SLACK IN THE LOINS**
Condition in which loins are weak – the last rib is short, with notice-able space between it and the hip.
- **SLIPHEAD**
Head strap and cheekpiece supporting the bradoon of a double bridle.
- **SLOW GAIT**
Slow, high-stepping, four-beat gait employed by Saddlebred horses.
- **SOUND HORSE**
Horse possessing a good frame, bodily health, and free from **blemishes**, defects, and "all impediments to sight and action."
- **SPLIT UP BEHIND**
Conformational fault caused by weakness of **gaskins**. Seen from behind, the thighs divide too high, just beneath the dock.
- **STALLION**
Uncastrated male horse four or more years old.
- **STAMP OF HORSE**
Type or pattern of horse.
- **STANDING OVER**
See **Over at the knee**.

- **STUDBOOK**
A book kept by a breed society in which the pedigrees of stock eligible for entry are recorded.
- **SUBSTANCE**
Physical quality of the body in terms of its build and general musculature.
- **TACK**
Riding and driving equipment.
- **THROAT LATCH**
Leather strap, part of the headpiece, that passes around the horse's throat.
- **TIED IN BELOW THE KNEE**
Condition in which the length below the knee is substantially less than that above the fetlock; or a conformational fault in which a horse is necessarily **light of bone**.
- **TOPLINE**
Line of the back from the withers to the end of the croup.
- **TYPE**
Horse that fulfils a particular purpose, like a cob, hunter, or hack, but does not necessarily belong to a specific breed.
- **UNDERSHOT**
Deformity in which the lower jaw projects beyond the upper.
- **UP TO WEIGHT**
A term describing a horse that, due to its substance, bone, size, and overall **conformation**, can carry a substantial weight.
- **WARMBLOOD**
In general terms, half- or part-bred horses, the result of Thoroughbred or Arabian crosses with other blood or bloods. *See also* **Coldblood**.
- **WEEDY**
Horse of poor, mean **conformation** carrying little flesh and often long-legged. Generally of Thoroughbred type.
- **WEIGHT CARRIER**
Horse capable of carrying 210 lb (95 kg). Also called a "heavyweight" horse.
- **WELL-SPRUNG RIBS**
Long, rounded ribs giving ample room for lung expansion and being well-suited to a saddle.
- **WHIP**
Driver of a carriage. Also an "artifical" **aid** used by the driver.
- **WOLF TEETH**
Rudimentary teeth occurring in front of the upper and lower molars on each side of the jaw. More usually found in upper jaw.

INDEX